THE SENSE
OF LEARNING

The Sense of Learning

Ann E. Berthoff

BOYNTON/COOK PUBLISHERS
HEINEMANN
PORTSMOUTH, NH

BOYNTON/COOK PUBLISHERS
A Division of
HEINEMANN EDUCATIONAL BOOKS
361 Hanover Street Portsmouth, NH 03801
Offices and agents throughout the world

The author would like to thank the following for granting permission to use material in this book:

Page v: "Statute" by Josephine Miles. From *Collected Poems: 1930–83* by Josephine Miles. Copyright © 1983 by Josephine Miles. Reprinted by permission of University of Illinois Press.

Versions of some of the chapters have been published previously:

Chapter 1: "Is Teaching Still Possible?" *College English*, 46:8 (December 1984). Copyright © 1984 by the National Council of Teachers of English. Reprinted by permission of the publisher.

Chapter 2: "Recognition, Representation, and Revision," *Journal of Basic Writing*, 3:3 (Fall/Winter 1981). Copyright © 1982, *Journal of Basic Writing*, Instructional Resource Center, Office of Academic Affairs, The City University of New York, 535 East 80 Street, New York, NY 10021. Reprinted by permission of the publisher.

Chapter 3: "Abstraction as a Speculative Instrument." This essay first appeared in *The Territory of Language*, ed. Donald McQuade (Carbondale: Southern Illinois University Press, 1986) and is reprinted with permission of Donald McQuade.

Chapter 4: "Is Learning Still Possible?" *Reclaiming the Classroom: Teacher Research as an Agency for Change*, ed. Dixie Goswami and Peter Stillman. Copyright © 1987 by Boynton/Cook Publishers, Inc. Reprinted by permission.

Chapter 8: "Is Reading Still Possible?" *Farther Along: Transforming Dichotomies in Rhetoric and Composition*, ed. Kate Ronald and Hephzibah Roskelly. Copyright © 1990 by Boynton/Cook Publishers, Inc. Reprinted by permission.

Chapter 9: "Reading the World . . . Reading the Word: Paulo Freire's Pedagogy of Knowing," *Only Connect: Uniting Reading and Writing*, ed. Thomas Newkirk. Copyright © 1986 by Boynton/Cook Publishers, Inc. Reprinted by permission.

Chapter 10: "Democratic Practice, Pragmatic Vistas: Louise Rosenblatt and the Reader's Response," appeared as "Louise Rosenblatt: Democratic Practice, Pragmatic Vistas" in *Reader*, 20 (Fall 1988). Copyright © 1988 by *Reader*. Reprinted by permission of the publisher.

Epilogue: "Ramus Meets Schleirmacher and They Go Off for a Triadic Lunch with Peirce; Vico Drops By," first appeared in *Discurrendo*. Reprinted by permission.

Library of Congress Cataloging-in-Publication Data

Berthoff, Ann E.
    The sense of learning / Ann E. Berthoff.
      p.   cm.
    Continues: The making of meaning. 1981.
    Includes bibliographical references.
    ISBN 0-86709-201-7
    1. English language—Rhetoric—Study and teaching. 2. Reading (Higher education) I. Berthoff, Ann E. Making of meaning. II. Title.
PE1404.B474 1990
808.042'07—dc20

                                      89–295087
                                         CIP

Designed by Vic Schwarz
Printed in the United States of America
90 91 92 93 94 9 8 7 6 5 4 3 2 1

IN MEMORIAM
JOSEPHINE MILES

The way I would look at the world, the houses
Take up half, the horizon
Moves straight across the view.
And the base half is houses, the roof lines of houses
Marking off the blue.

By what aerial license would it be possible
To promote any other line?
The piteous valley vista, or the terrible
Subordination
Seen by plane?

I would legislate against the Icarian downfall
As against the ascent of F6,
And take care
That the great legal skies of human vision
Observe their human shore.

("Statute," 1955)

Contents

Preface

This collection of essays, articles, addresses, and papers is a sequel to *The Making of Meaning: Metaphors, Models, and Maxims for Writing Teachers* (Boynton/Cook, 1981), offering further considerations of what it means to teach writing and reading as meaning-making activities. Two-thirds of these pieces have been published in journals and in collections of various sorts; the other third is constituted by occasional papers.

As headings for Parts I, II, and III and as titles of the initial pieces in each Part, I have posed three questions: *Is teaching still possible? Is learning still possible? Is reading still possible?* I found that I was raising these questions in my own mind because from the research reports I read and from most public commentary, it seemed that the clear answer was "NO! Education is no longer possible!" And that answer seemed ever more rational as I considered the solutions being offered: we must spend billions and billions of dollars; we must fund more programs designed by the Department of Education; we must have students with real moral fiber, developed either in the Sunday School of their choice or by seminars in values clarification; we must get back to basics, develop more and earlier and better testing; we must mandate national curricula, stress computer literacy, offer competency-based or real-life experience as educational options; etc. I have opinions on some of these matters, but I seldom offer them in this little book.

The questions I have raised are not presented as problems with suggested solutions: I have tried to pose problems, not to solve them. But I hold with I. A. Richards that if we look carefully at *what* we are trying to do, we will thereby discover *how* to do it.

In a Prologue, I have tried my hand at explaining the philosophy of language which has guided my problem posing. And in an Epilogue, I pay homage to certain heroic figures in the history of rhetoric and philosophy. There is scarcely a Monday-morning problem in teaching which does not have philosophical ramifications and, as I have long argued, we are philosophers whenever we recognize that that is so.

I have always held that practice without theory is foolish and that any theory is fatuous until it is brought to the test. *Reclaiming the Imagination*, an anthology I edited (Boynton/Cook, 1984), offers the kind of philosophical perspectives in which theories of composition and rhetoric are, I think, properly developed. *Forming/Thinking/Writing* (Second edition, prepared with the help of James E. Stephens, Boynton/Cook, 1988), provided the opportunity to bring my own theories to the test of practice. Those theories are all variants of an idea which has inspirited me from the moment I first entered a classroom forty years ago. The idea is that we are all language animals: Man is the *animal symbolicum*—which is to say that a species-specific or God-given capacity to make meaning is there in every student and that it is our duty as teachers to provide occasions for that capacity to be realized. The theories of knowledge, of learning, of interpretation, of forming which I have been elaborating for the past twenty-five years or so derive from the encounter of my teaching with my reading of (chiefly) Susanne K. Langer, Kenneth Burke, and I. A. Richards, of Coleridge, Whitehead, Cassirer, and Peirce.

Less austere than my bookish mentors, and ever so wise and warmhearted, was my friend Josephine Miles. She encouraged me in my endeavors in the field of composition pedagogy (as well as those in the study of Renaissance poetics) when I first met her in Berkeley in 1962 and, thereafter, with postcards and in brief conversations whenever I was in California. We discussed Wyatt and Marvell, linguistics and pedagogy, all with the same degree of intensity. One of the proudest moments of my professional life came when I heard that she had arranged to arrive at the conference of the California Association of Teachers of English in time to hear the luncheon address I was giving. And the fact that she liked what I had to say—in "The Teacher as REsearcher"—made me very happy indeed.

Jo's questions always startled me by the way they illuminated puzzling connections and awakened consciousness of others hitherto unrecognized. I believe that her four essays gathered in *Working Out Ideas: Predication and Other Uses of Language* set forth all we need in order to direct our pedagogical practice. And we have all benefited from her idea that university teachers and schoolteachers can learn from one another: that idea was a chief impetus for what was to become the Bay Area Writing Project. In gratitude for her kindness and her wisdom, I have dedicated these essays to the memory of Josephine Miles.

I have many other friends to thank, but rather than listing them, let me say to them all that I hope they'll approve of the arguments I have developed in these pieces; that they'll put any provocative ideas to the test in their own practice; that they'll let me know what they think about what happened. That goes for all my readers, for members of that interpretive community concerned to know what difference "the sense of learning" might make to their practice.

Concord, Massachusetts

Prologue

Learning from Signs

Learning from experience is a very familiar idea, but its significance depends on how we take it. If by *learning* we mean trial and error, negative reinforcement, and other such concepts of a behavioral psychology, we will be led in one direction; if by *learning* we mean a disposition to form structures (in Gordon Allport's definition), we will be led in another direction. In these essays, I am concerned to make a case for the second direction, toward a pedagogy of knowing and a theory of imagination as the forming power of the active mind, toward an understanding of language which can account for meaning and a rhetoric which is able to provide remedies for misunderstanding.

Forming structures is a semiotic activity: that is to say, it is the way we make meaning. Semiotics is the theory of signs, those forms by means of which we represent our interpretations of the world. If we want our composition theory to be directed toward writing as a mode of learning, we will need the guidance of a semiotics which can illuminate an understanding of "the sense of learning." My title comes from C. S. Peirce, the father of semiotics; what he meant by it can best be apprehended if we look at how he thought of representation and interpretation.

In recent years, I have often asked audiences of teachers and students to draw a diagram which I call "the curious tri-

1

angle." Its base is a dotted line; at the southwest angle is *symbol* (or *representamen*); at the southeast is *referent* (or *object*); and at the apex is *reference* (or *interpretant*). The dotted line is meant to indicate that the relationship of the signifier to what is signified can be understood only by means of a meaning which the interpreter has in mind. (Otherwise, you can't get there from here.) The curious triangle represents the meaning relationship as three-valued or *triadic*, instead of as a dyadic relationship holding between a signifier and a signified.

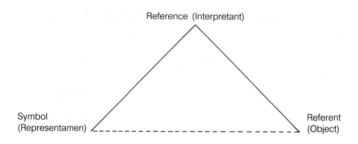

Reference (Interpretant)

Symbol
(Representamen)

Referent
(Object)

(The words in parentheses are Peirce's terms; the others are Ogden's and Richards's.)

The curious triangle made its first appearance in *The Meaning of Meaning,* by C. K. Ogden and I. A. Richards, in 1922. C. S. Peirce also made his first appearance outside philosophical journals in an appendix of this book. Ogden and Richards used the triangle with the dotted baseline to explain Peirce's triadic theory of the sign. *Triadicity*—the theory that there is a third element in the structure of the sign—puts the emphasis on the idea of meaning as a *means*.

I know of no evidence that Vygotsky had read either Peirce or Ogden and Richards, but the triangle with the dotted line appears (upside down) in a paper of his on play as mediated activity, first published in 1930 (*Reclaiming* 72).* And here is Northrop Frye using the curious triangle to explain another example of a triadic relationship:

The statement *Neptune is the sea* is the baseline of a triangle whose apex points to a group of worshippers whose cult is organized around saying so.

---

*See note in Works Cited.

For all of us, the curious triangle can represent the idea that when we make meaning, we think not just *about* meanings but *with* them. You can't get from a-p-p-l-e p-i-e to the edible object directly; there is no reason whatsoever that the sounds represented by those letters (or the letters themselves) should mean the pie-as-object. The conventions of language make it possible for them to do so in the first place, but we have to have an idea of apple pie in mind, to say nothing of ideas of apple and pie, if we are to understand what is being said.

Most of the essays in this book explore in one way or another these two aspects of language and how they are related: language is both a formal system and a symbolic form; language is at once "grammar" and "meaning," and we couldn't have one without the other. The formal system is the necessary but not the sufficient condition of expression and communication: those symbolic functions would be impossible without the formal system, but that is not to say that the system and its functions are identical. Cassirer spoke of the two tasks of language: the universal logical task and the social task. When we teach writing as a mode of learning and a way of knowing, we will need to remember the interdependence of the two tasks, recognizing that they are not the same, while understanding, too, that they are not separable in the real world of expression and communication. The two tasks do not stand in an antithetical relationship to each other; they are dialectically related. It is in considering this dialectic that we figure out how to relate what is said to what is (probably) meant. And that is why I. A. Richards called *dialectic* "the audit of meaning."

Another dialectical relationship we must recognize in our teaching is the one holding between the logical and the psychological aspects of interpretation. Triadicity, the idea of meaning as a three-valued relationship, guarantees a logical place for interpretation: that's the Third. Just as there could be no symbolic representation without the formal system provided by language, so the sign would not function if we didn't include interpretation. That's what it means to say that mediation is logically dependent on the *idea* held by the interpreter; that's why Peirce preferred to speak of the *interpretant* rather than the *interpreter*. (In his later years, he conflated them, as "a Sop to Cerberus.") The necessary condition of interpretation is the logical role of the interpretant, the idea which mediates between the symbol and what it represents. But, of course, the sufficient condition is the individual interpreter who holds the idea and makes meaning with it. Thus, the interdependence of the logical and the psychological aspects of interpretation is analogous to the interdependence of the two tasks of language.[1]

The chief consequence of mediation is that we must interpret our interpretations. Without direct access to reality, there is no guarantee that we're right, so we must cultivate, Peirce held, "a contrite fallibilism." As we continually interpret our interpretations, the Interpretant of one sign becomes the Representamen of the next, which will have a new Interpretant. (This is the meaning of Peirce's most famous formulation, that each sign requires another for its interpretation.) We can represent that process diagrammatically by triangles which become curiouser and curiouser.

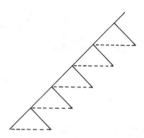

Logically speaking, there is no end to this process of thinking about our thinking, but since we live not within the confines of a syllogism but in the real world, with real purposes and the real constraints of time and space, we must bring the process to a halt: we interrupt the interpretation of interpretation by asking *"If we put it this way, what difference would it make to our practice?"* This "pragmatic maxim" is the method of pragmatism in slogan form. Peirce did not mean by his pragmatism being hard-nosed or cost-conscious or "realistic." Pragmatism—which Peirce renamed *pragmaticism* when he decided that William James had misunderstood what he meant—means judging an opinion or a theory or an alleged fact by its consequences. And it means continuing the process of interpreting whatever representation we make of our thoughts and feelings by seeing the difference it *actually* makes.

Peirce's pragmaticism is entailed in his triadic semiotics. If we give up the idea of positive knowledge by means of a direct access to reality, adopting instead the conception of knowledge as interpretation, then we must have a way of bringing our hypotheses to the test. Pragmaticism was intended to provide both the rationale and the method for doing just that.

The questions posed in this book—*Is teaching still possible? Is learning still possible? Is reading still possible?*—are meant as points of departure for an exploration of what it means to teach, to learn, to read. If we let the idea of triadicity guide us, the possibilities are endless. If we make interpretation central in our teaching (as it is in all knowing), it will be central in our students' learning. As interpretations are interpreted, students learn how to make the powers of language a resource in their reading and writing. Language is itself heuristic, but that power will not be accessible if it is presented as a series of slots to be filled or a rack of garments to be used for clothing thoughts. If language is considered, as I. A. Richards put it, a verbal butterfly net with which we catch nonverbal butterflies, there will be no way to make reading and writing modes of learning. The way to assure that they are is to be guided by a philosophy of language that makes interpretation central. The generative powers of language are evident as we observe how representations are interpreted, how interpretations are to be represented. Meaning emerges in that process and, as it is reflected upon, reconsidered, revised, and represented anew, everybody learns.

For Peirce, this process of interpreting signs—the habit of reflecting on interpretations, of drawing out implications of one or another representation; the "plural consciousness" which allows differing interpretations to be formulated and brought to the test—he called *the sense of learning*. If "learning from experience" is understood as what Peirce called "the endless process of learning from signs," I think we can invent humane pedagogies which will endlessly create possibilities for teaching and learning.

Note

1. For a discussion of this concept, see Ann E. Berthoff, "Sapir and the Two Tasks of Language," *Semiotica*, 71-1/2 (1988), 1–47.

I

Is Teaching Still Possible?

Yes—if it is conceived as dialogic action in classrooms which are philosophic laboratories for the study of meaning.

*   *   *

Eric Havelock claimed that Socrates was put to death because he attempted to replace apprenticeship with instruction. The history of education might be seen as a perennial contest between the two, but in any case what we mean by either apprenticeship or instruction will be determined by our semiotics—by how we account for the making of meaning.

If we think of meaning as thing-y or as something to be ingested, then instruction will be a matter of handing over the facts or the wisdom, and apprenticeship will mean studying how to do what somebody else does in order to copy it, mastering procedures and practices without any necessary concern for purpose. All that we might consider representative of the apprenticeship model—peer groups, free writing, an emphasis on process—the efficacy of anything we might consider the achievement of a humane pedagogy depends on the place we find for interpretation. In the triadic perspective, all knowledge is interpretation and teaching, a hermeneutic enterprise. Because triadicity fosters the idea of meaning as emergent in a process of determination, it guides us toward an appreciation of apprenticeship as a mode of learning at once critical and creative, capable of fully engaging the imagination.

Attitudes toward instruction are likewise contingent on our semiotics. It would seem obvious that instruction in itself is neither good nor bad since it depends on how it is carried out, but an idea currently gaining acceptance is that since teaching divides instructor from instructed, it is necessarily oppressive. The technocratic solution is to turn instruction over to machines or their surrogates, teachers who follow programmed textbooks. The postmodern solution is to deny the idea of instruction altogether—which is why we commonly find "radical" teachers who haven't a clue about how to lead a discussion, who generally are happy to return to lecturing, and "conservative" teachers who think that the way to encourage dialogue is by simply asking "What do *you* think?"

If we equip ourselves with the speculative instruments which triadicity provides—ideas to think *with*—we can successfully reclaim both instruction and apprenticeship. I believe that if we make interpretation central in our teaching, anything we do will have heuristic value—even sentence combining. Further, I would argue that if interpretation remains defined in reductive psychological terms, nothing we do will enable or empower our students.

1

Is Teaching Still Possible?

In the memorable disquisition with which he begins *Permanence and Change*, Kenneth Burke explains how thinking which does not include thinking about thinking is merely problem solving, an activity carried out very well by trouts.

> Though all organisms are critics in the sense that they interpret the signs about them, the experimental speculative technique made available by speech would seem to single out the human species as the only one possessing an equipment for going beyond the criticism of experience to a criticism of criticism. We not only interpret the characters of events. . . . We may also interpret our interpretations (pp. 5–6).

That species-specific capacity for thinking about thinking, for interpreting interpretations, for knowing our knowledge, is, I think, the chief resource for any teacher and the ground of hope in the enterprise of teaching reading and writing.

I plan to be cheerful but there is a certain amount of setting aside which needs to be done before I can confidently

Closing address at the Third National Institute on the Relationships Among Intellectual Development, Critical Thinking, and Effective Writing Across the Curriculum at the University of Chicago, November 1983. Published in *College English* (1984).

claim that teaching is still possible. About half my time will go to nay-saying: I want first to assess the hazards of developmental models and the positivist views of language which underwrite them. I will turn then to a consideration of how alternative views of language and learning can help us invent a pedagogy that views reading and writing as interpretation and the making of meaning.

What we have these days is properly described, I think, as a pedagogy of exhortation: "Feel comfortable. . . . Wake up! . . . Find something you're interested in. . . . Get your thesis statement. . . . Say what you really think. . . . Go over your paper and take out all unnecessary words." But exhortation, whether left-wing or right-wing, is not instructive. (No writer ever puts in words which he thinks are unnecessary; learning to discover that some *are* is one of the chief challenges in learning to write.) What must supplant the pedagogy of exhortation is a "pedagogy of knowing." The phrase is Paulo Freire's, and he means by it what Socrates, Maria Montessori, Jane Addams, I. A. Richards, Roger Ascham, or other great teachers would have meant, namely, that unless and until the mind of the learner is engaged, no meaning will be made, no knowledge can be won.

What chiefly forestalls our moving from a pedagogy of exhortation to a pedagogy of knowing is a dependence on a view of language which cannot account *for* meaning or give an account *of* meanings. A positivist conception of language as a "communication medium," as a set of muffin tins into which the batter of thought is poured, leads to question-begging representations and models of the composing process. Understanding what a pedagogy of knowing would involve is prevented by an unhealthy confusion about what development means and a damaging dependence on the stage models which cognitive psychologists have elaborated, supposedly for the benefit of rhetoricians as well as for guidance counselors, therapists, curriculum designers, and the publishers of values clarification kits.

Let me begin with a passage from an article by a rhetorician who is discussing cross-disciplinary programs.

Since the early 1970s evidence has been accumulating which suggests that up to fifty percent of the adolescent population in this country fail to make the transition from the concrete operational stage to formal operations by the time they have reached late high school or college age. Judging from this empirical research, it would appear that as many as half of our students from junior high on into adulthood are unable to think abstractly, to process and produce logical propositions (Freisinger, 163).

Three points are notable: First, the Piagetian model, which is of course intended to represent the stages of development of the language and thought of the child, is here applied to the reasoning of young adults; second, "empirical research" is taken as providing evidence in support of certain claims about learning; third, the failure to reach the stage of formal operations is made equivalent to an inability to "think abstractly," which, in turn, is identified as processing and producing logical propositions. These are all misconceptions. The attempt to apply the Piagetian stage model to non-children is futile; the claim that empirical research supports the efficacy of doing so is false; the identification of abstract thought with processing propositions begs the question of what constitutes that process.

What the child does or does not do may look like what the incompetent or deficient or uneducated adult does or does not do, but it does not follow that the two instances are alike so far as motivation or function is concerned. Just so, the savage is not a child; the lunatic is not a poet; the chimp who has been taught sign language cannot be said to be using it as either the hearing or deaf human being does. To see the similarities without noting the differences is to settle for pseudo-concepts, in Vygotsky's phrase.

If we do form a concept of language as not just a medium of communication but a means of making meaning, we preclude a dependence on empirical research to find out what is happening in our classrooms, to see what writers do when they compose. If you start with a working concept of language as a means of making meaning, you are recognizing that language can be studied only by means of language. Understood in such terms as *context, purpose, intention, import, reference, significance, ambiguity, representation,* and so on, linguistic structures or texts or speech acts can be studied only by interpreting the interdependencies of meanings—and by interpreting our interpretations. But if these conceptions are central, what is there for empirical researchers to investigate? Empiricists do not generally recognize that all method, including scientific method, entails interpretation; they do not generally recognize that there are no raw data; there are no self-sufficient facts; there is no context-free evaluation. Their method is not to recognize the fact that all knowledge is mediated and that facts must be formulated, but to proceed as if interpretation were supererogatory. Empirical researchers leave out of account meaning because they have no means of accounting for it. I. A. Richards observed of this kind of investigator that he "does not know how to respect the language."

> He does not yet have a conception of the language which would make it respectable. He thinks of it as a code and has not yet learned that it is an organ—the supreme organ of the mind's self-ordering growth. Despite all his claims to be expert in collecting, reporting, comparing, and systematizing linguistic facts, he has not yet apprehended the greatest of them all: that language is an instrument for controlling our becoming (*Speculative* 9).[1]

Some of the human sciences have seen the folly of denying the very subject which should be at the heart of the study of the language animal, the *animal symbolicum*. The anthropologist Clifford Geertz, in a wonderful essay called "Thick Description," shows just what it means to ask questions about what human beings are doing (*Reclaiming* 226–248). He undertakes to explain how context and perspective function in interpretation by subjecting an example of Gilbert Ryle's to analysis: A boy is seen to wink; another boy has a tic which involves his eyelid; a third boy is seen practicing an imitation of the boy with the tic. Try describing these "behaviors," as the empirical researcher would call them, and watch two of them become human acts, motivated and meaningful—and subject to interpretation.

If meaning is set aside in the search for "data," the findings will not then be applicable to the making of meaning. But composition specialists who follow psycholinguistic principles of analysis want to have it both ways: their empirical research requires that meaning be left out of account, but they also want to claim that their findings are relevant to pedagogy. What writers do is thus confused with what psycholinguists want to study. This methodological pitfall is impossible to avoid when the investigator is guided by a conception of language as a code.

The empiricist needs something to measure, and cohesive devices can be counted, once there is a taxonomy. They are a feature of discourse analysis, which is not, as one might have thought, a matter of studying the dialectic of what-is-said and what-is-meant; it is not the analysis of intention and recalcitrant linguistic structures in dialectic, the relationship that makes the representation of meaning possible; it is by no means simply a fancy name for "critical reading": discourse analysis is the study of "information management," "thematic structure," "sentence rules," and, preeminently, of "cohesion." Now the "cohesiveness" of a text is not the same thing as "coherence." Coherence is mentalistic; it isn't there on the page; it cannot be measured and graphed; it can only be interpreted in terms of the emergent meanings of the writer. But for the psycholinguistic investigator, it is not writers who produce texts; texts are created by cohesive devices.

At a recent conference I heard a psycholinguist explain how, in order to foreground the cohesive devices, he had to reduce the role of meaning. The first problem in the design of his experiment was to find a passage or a stretch of discourse in which meaning was not important so that it would be easier to measure the responsiveness of college students to cohesive devices. He spent some time in preparing the text, but I wondered why he didn't simply excise something from any textbook in any discipline published in any year, since they are generally written so that readers will not be irritated or distracted by the need to interpret what is being said in an attempt to understand what was intended.

This kind of empirical research institutionalizes the pedagogy of exhortation: "Does your paper flow? If not, check your transitions. Can your reader follow you? Be sure to give him clues." Thus we get papers full of roadsigns, often pointing in the wrong direction—*however,* when there is no *however* relationship; *on the other hand,* introducing a faulty parallel; redundancy (the uninstructed writer's only means of emphasis); end linkages—which I call Nixonian Syntactic Ligature—with the beginning of each sentence picking up the exact wording of the end of the preceding sentence. Research on cohesive devices easily seeps into composition theory because it sounds scientific and because anything that lets us count will seem helpful in evaluating what we think we are teaching. But the fact that cohesive ties may be identified and classified can easily distract us from the problem of learning how to help writers discover, in the very act of realizing their intentions, the discursive power of language itself, what Edward Sapir meant by calling language heuristic. Empirical research into "discourse acquisition" is likely, I think, to mislead us—to lead us away from thinking about thinking, to keep us from studying the process whereby writers discover the resources of language and learn to control them in the making of meaning.[2]

The challenge to experimental design should be not to reduce meaning or to try to eliminate it; this is a primitive conception of what disembedding involves. The challenge to experimental design is not to dispense with meaning but to control language so that there are not too many meanings at a time; so that the learners can discern, in I. A. Richards' words, "the partially parallel task" (*Speculative* 96) when they confront it; so that the teacher, by means of a careful sequence of lessons or assignments, can assure that the students are conscious of their minds in action, can develop their language by means of exercising deliberate choice. Positivists see no virtue whatsoever in consciousness of consciousness since they model conceptualization on motor skills—and everybody knows that there consciousness becomes self-consciousness: you'll fall off the bicycle if you think hard about what you're doing. What is forgotten is that wherever language is concerned we are dealing with symbolic acts. Consciousness there is not that "self" consciousness which is so destructive but Freire's "conscientization" or Burke's "interpretation of our interpretations" or Richards' "comprehending our comprehensions more comprehensively" or Coleridge's "knowing our knowledge" or Cassirer's "confrontation of an act of awareness" and so on. Consciousness of consciousness is entailed in our activity as language animals.

If psychologists would read Susanne K. Langer's *Mind: An Essay on Human Feeling*, they would have a clearer idea of what they are about. Or they could read a little phenomenology, but psychology is usually about a generation behind. Thus psychologists have recently taken up structuralism, just as it's being laid to rest elsewhere. And before that it was operationalism, which fed itself on hard data. Robert Oppenheimer, in a brilliant talk to the American Psychological Association in 1955, urged the members not to mimic a determinist physics "which is not there any more" (*Reclaiming* 189–202). He suggested, rather, that they listen to a man named Jean Piaget. Nowadays, when psychology is awash in Piagetian concepts, it is hard to imagine that this warning was necessary, but Oppenheimer realized that those in charge were the successors to those whom William James had called "brass instrument psychologists." Oppenheimer said: "I make this plea not to treat too harshly those who tell you a story, having observed carefully without having established that they are sure that the story is the whole story and the general story" (201).

The story Piaget had to tell was certainly interesting, but it isn't the whole story or the general story, and some psychologists, by examining Piaget's experimental designs very carefully, have shown how and where he went wrong. I call your attention to an excellent little book, *Children's Minds*, by Margaret Donaldson. She is neither polemical about Piaget nor worshipful of some anti-Piaget. Dozens of experiments are described which offer alternative explanations of children's responses to certain questions and situations designed to test their cognitive skills. They clearly establish that Piaget's findings, in instance after instance, are the artifacts of his procedures. The alleged incapacity to "decenter" is seen to be a matter of difficulty in locomotion and movement and not in a lack of "object concept" or an incapacity to entertain other points of view. It seems clear that children who made "egocentric" responses in various experiments of Piaget did not fully understand what they were supposed to do.

Margaret Donaldson writes in one of the summaries:

> Children are not at any stage as egocentric as Piaget has claimed . . . [they] are not so limited in ability to reason deductively as Piaget—and others—have claimed. . . . There is no reason to suppose that [the child] is born with an "acquisitive device" which enables him to structure and make sense of the language he hears while failing to structure and make sense of the other features of his environment (55–56).

The recent corrective experiments she discusses are fascinating, but there are precedents. What Margaret Donaldson's psychologists have done for the semantics and syntax of Piagetian questions, Rudolf Arnheim did for visual representation in Piagetian problems. Ever alert to the powers of visual thinking, Arnheim illustrates what he calls "visual illiteracy" with a pair of drawings in cross section of a water tap in open and closed position, schematic representations used in one of Piaget's perceptual problems. In a series of devastating questions in *Visual Thinking* he points out the ambiguities and concludes as follows:

> I am not denying that a person, immunized and warned by years of exposure to mediocre textbook illustrations, mail order catalogues, and similar products of visual ineptness, can figure out the meaning of these drawings, especially if helped by verbal explanation. But surely, if a child passes the test he does so in spite of the drawing, not with the help of it; and if he fails, he has not shown that he does not understand the working of a tap. He may simply be unable to extricate himself from a visual pitfall (312).

But of course the centrally important critique of Piaget's work came from Lev Vygotsky as early as 1932. Vygotsky's strictures concern not only the relationship of language and thought but also that of learning and instruction.[3] All study of language and thought, Vygotsky argued, must begin with the "unit of meaning," since neither language as element nor thought as element can be apprehended in its real character without the context provided by the other. Speech is not articulated sound plus intention; it is not speech until and unless it is meaningful. Neither language nor thought is meaningful outside a social context—which is to say that purpose and intention are from the first constrained not by a need for "communication" but by a need for representation, which of course invites and demands interpretation. Language is symbolic activity and from the first establishes itself in a social setting. The crucial difference between Vygotsky's procedures and Piaget's is that language is built into Vygotsky's test design and the tester is actively involved in exchanges with the subject. Piaget, Vygotsky thought, did not appreciate the complex dialectic of the learning curve and the role of instruction. The explanation for the misleading questions and the ambiguous directions is to be sought in the fact that Piaget thought that the only way to test cognitive skills was to isolate them as far as possible from language-dependent settings. The failure to understand the interdependence of language and thought is consonant with the misconception of the role of instruction which, like test design, is considered by Piaget in mechanistic terms.

Why should we care about Piaget and his critics? Don't we have enough to do, taking care of course design and teacher training and writing across the curriculum and trying to assure the survival of departments of English and to assuage deans who are counting FTE's—don't we have enough to do without worrying over arguments which may or may not be intelligible or important? The answer is that if we don't understand the grounds for a critical appraisal of theories of cognitive development, if we let our practice be guided by whatever we are told has been validated by empirical research, we will get what we have got: a conception of learning as contingent on development in a straightforward, linear fashion; of development as a preset program which is autonomous and does not require instruction; of language as words used as labels; of meaning as a one-directional, one-dimensional attribute; of the human mind as an adaptive mechanism. Thus are we wrecked on the rocks of teaching seen as intervention; of the so-called student-centered classroom; of single-skill correction; of discourse analysis, in which the chief function of discourse is disregarded; of reading instruction in which language is considered solely as a graphic code; of writing seen as the assignment of topics sequenced according to the commonplaces of classical rhetoric, as interpreted by associationist psychology: narrative before description, compare-contrast separate from definition, expression way before exposition; an affective English 101 (Turn off your mind and float downstream!) and a cognitive English 102 (Get your thesis statement! Generalize! Be brief! Don't generalize!).

Developmental models uncritically deployed lead to the kind of judgment exemplified in the final sentence of the text I took as my point of departure, the one stating that students can't think abstractly, that they can't "produce or process logical propositions." We should not be surprised that this writer goes on to say that "It is fairly obvious from work done in psychology that we cannot accelerate the transition from concrete to formal operations." What is surprising is the rest of the sentence: "but we may be able to promote its natural development by creating a more natural classroom environment" (Freisinger, p. 163). Why would we aim to promote its "natural development" if we don't think we can "accelerate the transition" to a stage now long overdue? Yet I am cheered by this absurd contradiction, cheered according to the same logic by which Gide was led to praise hypocrisy as a step in the right direction. I think the writer is a better teacher than the theory he explicitly depends on lets him be; so he discards it! He finds another which allows him to speak of promoting natural development in a natural environment. That sounds like somebody who believes that teaching is still possible!

I am now ready to be cheerful. The first piece of good news is that what college students find difficult—what everybody finds difficult, what diplomats and doctors of medicine and of philosophy find difficult—is not *abstraction* but *generalization*. These acts of mind are conflated by positivists, but they are not the same. Abstraction is not generalization. This is not a quibble; if it were, our enterprise would be futile and the very idea of education fatuous.

Abstraction is natural, normal: it is the way we make sense of the world in perception, in dreaming, in all expressive acts, in works of art, in all imagining. Abstraction is the work of the active mind; it is what the mind does as it forms. The name for this power of mind used to be imagination. We do not have to teach it: it is the work of our Creator. It is a God-given power or, if you prefer, it is a specific power the *animal symbolicum* has in lieu of a repertory of instincts which obviate the necessity of interpreting interpretations. We do not have to teach abstraction. What we do have to do is to show students how to reclaim their imaginations so that "the prime agent of all human perception" can be for them a living model of what they do when they write. What we must learn to do, if we are to move from the pedagogy of exhortation to a pedagogy of knowing, is to show students how to use what they already do so cleverly in order to learn how to generalize—how to move from abstraction in the nondiscursive mode to discursive abstraction, to generalization. We must strive to "raise implicit recognitions to explicit differentiations": that phrase comes from a book called *The Philosophy of Rhetoric*, published nearly fifty years ago by I. A. Richards. We do not yet have a philosophy of rhetoric, for the very good reason that we, teachers of reading and writing and those responsible for literacy at all levels, have not "taken charge of the criticism of our own assumptions," as Richards urged. The second piece of good news is that there is a semiotics which can guide that enterprise.

It starts from a triadic rather than a dyadic conception of the sign.[4] Triadicity is an idea whose time has surely come. It can help us take charge of the criticism of our assumptions about teaching because in the triadic conception of the sign, the symbol user, the knower, the learner is integral to the process of making meaning. The curious triangle, by thus representing the mediating function of interpretation, can serve as an emblem for a pedagogy of knowing. Indeed, my third piece of good news is that triadicity can help us reclaim imagination and the idea of language as "the supreme organ of the mind's self-ordering growth." I will conclude now with a sketch of this view of language and how it can lead us toward an authentic pedagogy of knowing.

Language seen as a means of making meaning has two aspects, the hypostatic and the discursive. By naming the world, we hold images in mind; we remember; we can return to our experience and reflect on it. In reflecting, we can change, we can transform, we can envisage. Language thus becomes the very type of social activity by which we might move toward changing our lives. The hypostatic power of language to fix and stabilize frees us from the prison of the moment. Language recreates us as historical beings. In its discursive aspect language runs along and brings thought with it, as Cassirer puts it. Discourse grows from inner dialogue (and the differing accounts by Piaget and Vygotsky of that development make a fascinating study). From this earliest activity of the mind, language gradually takes on the discursive forms which serve the communicative function. Because of this tendency to syntax, we can articulate our thoughts; we can think about thinking and thus interpret our interpretations.

Seeing language in this perspective encourages the recognition that meaning comes first; that it is complex from the start; that its articulation is contingent on the mind's activity in a human world. The chief hazard of the developmental model is that it sanctions the genetic fallacy—that what comes first is simple, not complex, and that what comes after is a bigger version of a little beginning. Thus we have the idea that there is first one word and then another, another, another, until there is enough to fill out the awaiting syntactic structures. But this isn't the way it happens. The hypostatic word, the single uttered syllable, is a proto-sentence; syntax is deeply implicated, we might say, in every human cry. Children let a single word do the work of the sentence until the discursive power of language can draw out and articlate the meaning. The conception of a semantic component added to a syntactic structure is a mechanistic conception which must be supplanted. I suggest as an image of the growth and development of language one of those little wooden flowers which the Japanese used to make —before they turned to silicon chips—a tiny compacted form which, placed in a dish of water, opens and expands, blossoming in the shape of a fully articulated flower. Please note the dialectic: it is the water which acts to release the form. In my extended metaphor, the water is our social life, the essential context for the making of meaning. Cognitive psychologists who deliberately ignore it have not advanced over those early kings whose hobby it was to try to discover which language is oldest. They sequestered newborn twins in castle keep or cottage, in the care of a mute nurse, and breathlessly awaited news of what language it would be, when the babies came to speak. And you can safely bet that the court astrologer—that proto-psycholinguist—saw to it that the first reported syllables were construed as Swedish or Hebrew or whatever language it was that the monarch—that proto-funding agency—expected.

In my opinion, the ambiguities of the determinism suggested by any account of natural, normal development can serve as the hinges of our thinking about thinking in the interest of discovering the laws of growth, the interdependency of nature and nurture, seed and soil. Language and learning, like syntax and semantics, are in a dialectical relationship which we must learn to construe and represent so that it is accessible to our students. Just so, we must guide their consciousness of consciousness so that it can become the means of freeing the self from itself: as a pleasant way of resolving that paradox, I recommend Walker Percy's *Lost in the Cosmos: The Last Self-Help Book*. After a startling and instructive analysis of twenty versions of the lost self, we have a chapter on triadicity, the means of reclaiming the self. Dr. Percy is an artist, a scientist, and a philosopher for whom triadicity provides the means of conceiving that symbolic activity which defines the mind.

Because they make interpretation central, triadic models of the composing process are the trustworthy ones we need in developing a pedagogy of knowing. The two I consider most useful are perception and dialogue. Every course I teach begins with observation—with looking and looking again. It is my strong conviction that what is looked at should include organic objects, themselves compositions. But, of course, we must also "problematize the existential situation," as Freire rather infelicitously puts it. I bring seaweed and crab legs to class, the seed pods of sedges and five kinds of pine cones, but I also ask students to problematize the soda cans and milk cartons left from the last class.[5] (I haven't dared to undertake the archeology of the wastebasket: God knows what we might find!) We use my version of the journalist's heuristic, *HDWDWW?*—deliberately constructed to resist becoming an acronym: *How does who do what and why?* How does that come to be on your desk? Who left it there? Why do you leave this junk around? What are these things in evidence of? What is the meaning of this litter? Looking and looking again helps students learn to transform things into questions; they learn to see names as "titles for situations," as Kenneth Burke puts it. In looking and naming, looking again and renaming, they develop perspectives and contexts, discovering how each controls the other. They are composing; they are forming; they are abstracting.

Perception is nondiscursive abstraction; the questioning of perceptions is the beginning of generalization, of discursive abstraction. Perception as a model of the composing process lets us capitalize on the hypostatic function of language. Students can discover that they are already thinking; by raising implicit recognitions to explicit differentiations, they can, as it were, *feel* the activity of their minds. By beginning with meaning, with complexity, we assure that minds will, indeed, be active. As I've been arguing, that complexity must be controlled by the way we use language or it will overwhelm, but the complexity entailed in making meaning should never be put off: *elements of what we want to end with must be present in some form from the first or we will never get to them.* That, I take it, is the chief law of growth.

Dialogue is the other triadic model. The "natural environment" necessary to the growth and development of the discursive power of language requires dialogue. Looking again starts that questioning which is the beginning of dialectic and it should be practiced in dialogue in class, of course, but also in what I call a "dialectical notebook," the facing pages offering a structure which enables the student to talk to himself. Dialogue is essential not only because it provides practice in those other uses of language—speaking and listening—but because it can model that constant movement from the particular to the general and back again which for Vygotsky is the defining characteristic of concept formation. But let me be explicit about this natural environment: it is a *prepared* environment, in the sense in which Montessori spoke of her classroom as a prepared environment. This dialectic of particularizing and generalizing, this conceptualizing, this thinking, though it is a power natural by reason of language itself, though it is natural to the human mind, must be put into practice. Like speech itself, it requires a social context in which purposes can be arrived at, intentions discovered and formulated and represented in different modes of discourse.

If college students find generalizing difficult, it's because nobody has ever taught them how to go about it, and abstraction which proceeds by means of generalizing—*concept formation*, as it is often called—must be deliberately learned and should therefore be deliberately taught. But few methods for doing so have been developed and those which have are, generally speaking, of the type Freire calls the banking model: the teacher deposits valuable information. Developmental models are most dangerous when they distract teachers from recognizing the deficiencies of their pedagogy. When we are told, as we are by almost everybody reporting research, that students are good at narrative but fall apart when faced with exposition, it is not necessary to hypothesize that students have come bang up against a developmental fence. The first step of the analysis should be to look at the character of the assignments, at the sequence of "tasks." In an interesting variation on this theme of "narrative good, exposition terrible," one researcher contrasts how well students do with persuasion and how poorly they do with argument.[6] She reports how intelligently students have jumped through the hoops of compare-contrast, "explain a process," "describe an incident," etc.—all in the interest of composing in the persuasive mode—only to fall flat on their faces with the argumentation paper. And guess where it came from? Not from exploration or dialogue or observation or a close reading of texts. No: it came from an assigned topic on euthanasia. Why is anybody surprised when they get terrible writing from a terrible assignment? "Who is to get the kidney machine?" is no advance at all over "Which is greater, fire or water?" "Provocative" topics stimulate cant and cliché; they breed "Engfish"; they lead to debate, which is by no means dialectic. Nobody learns from debate because, as Richards often observed, the disputant is commonly too busy making a point to trouble to see what it is.

Assigning topics—the essential strategy of the pedagogy of exhortation—is no substitute for instruction. But the deeper reason for the failure in the argumentation paper is the same as for the proclaimed success in the persuasion paper. Persuasion is the air we breathe; it is the mode of advertisement. But where do our students hear argument? Mine do not have the faintest idea of the conventions of an editorial—and when have they ever heard an authentic, dialectical exchange on television information shows? The discourse we find familiar to the point of being able to reproduce it has nothing to do with developmental stages, once childhood is passed—or maybe even before. You may be sure that prepubescent Presbyterians in the eighteenth century were capable of composing arguments on natural depravity, while prepubescent Baptists were writing on grace abounding unto the chief of sinners, and little Methodists were writing on topics like "Must the drunkard be an unhappy man?" My advanced composition students find almost intolerably difficult Huxley's "On a Piece of Chalk," a public lecture which a century ago famously enthralled workers with no secondary education—but Huxley's audience had heard two or three sermons every week of their lives! Argument was the air you breathed, a hundred years ago. I am not, of course, claiming authenticity or moral superiority for those who can argue. I mean only that the capacity to manage disputation is a culture-bound skill and that its dependence on neurobiological development is a necessary but not a sufficient condition.

Ironically, it is sometimes students themselves who misconceive the developmental model. Especially older students fear that they must return to Square One. They have to make it all up, they think.[7] When we ask them, like everybody else, to look and look again, we must, by a careful choice of reading—on the model of malt whiskey, not diet soda—lead them to discover that scientists and lawyers and poets look and look again. Of course we must "begin with where they are"—as meaning makers. We must, in I. A. Richards' phrase, offer them "assisted invitations" to look carefully at what they are doing—observing a weed or drawing up a shopping list—in order to discover *how* to do it. Our job is to devise sequences of assignments which encourage conscientization, the discovery of the mind in action. That will not be accomplished by setting topics, no matter how nicely matched to the "appropriate" developmental stage they might be.

Rather, in our pedagogy of knowing, we will encourage the discovery of mind by assuring that language is seen not as a set of slots, not as an inert code to be mastered by drill, but as a means of *naming* the world; of holding the images by whose means we human beings recognize the forms of our experience; of reflecting on those images, as we do on other words. We teachers will assure that language is continually exercised to name and establish likes and differents so that by sorting and gathering, students will learn to define: they will learn to abstract in the discursive mode; they will learn to generalize. They will thus be able to "think abstractly" because they will be learning how meanings make further meanings possible, how form finds further form. And we will, in our pedagogy of knowing, be giving our students back their language so that they can reclaim it as an instrument for controlling their becoming.

Notes

1. It is the lack of a philosophy of language that could properly account for meaning which invalidates the procedures so frequently recommended for students of the composing process. George Hillocks, for instance, suggests that inquiry procedures are well modeled by ethology. (See his article "Inquiry and the Composing Process: Theory and Research," *College English,* 44[1982], 659–73.) But as Susanne K. Langer has shown in the second volume of *Mind: An Essay on Human Feeling* (Baltimore, MD: Johns Hopkins University Press, 1972), Frisch, Tinbergen, et al. are unaware of the role metaphor plays in their descriptions; of presuppositions which remain entirely unexamined; of distortions resulting from a failure to differentiate animal and human acts. Ethological interpretations are shown to be pseudo-concepts, generalizations about particular cases, not authentic concepts.

2. I do not deny the value of analyzing cohesive devices in the context of discourse; this, I take it, is precisely what Richards had in mind when he called rhetoric "the study of how words work." But "discourse analysis," as presently practiced, does not always take into account the interdependence of linguistic and rhetorical functions. It begs the question of the relationship of language and thought, because the positivist conception of language by which it is guided does not provide the means for accounting for meaning. Discourse analysts separate thinking from writing, which they conceive of as the manipulation of *devices.* When Charles R. Cooper tells us in "Procedures for Describing Written Texts" (in *Research on Writing,* ed. Peter Mosenthal and Shaun Walmsley [New York: Longman, 1983]) that the "thinking process leads the writer to choose appropriate strategies and forms for presenting the outcomes of thought *as written text*" (p. 291), he has not been alert to those hazards Vygotsky urges us to avoid by beginning with the unit of meaning. For Professor Cooper it is clearly not part of the procedure for describing, much less for producing, "texts" to take into ac-

count the heuristic powers of language or the interplay of feedback and what Richards calls "feedforward."

It should be noted that for Halliday and Hasan, whose taxonomy is widely used, the working concept of a text is as a semantic unit. For an excellent discussion of the interdependence of meaning and grammatical, logical, and rhetorical forms, see Jeanne Fahnestock, "Semantic and Lexical Coherence," *College Composition and Communication*, 34 (1983), 400–16. And see anything Josephine Miles ever wrote.

3. See especially "Development of Scientific Concepts in Childhood" in *Thought and Language*, trans. and ed. Eugenia Hanfman and Gertrude Vakar (Cambridge, MA: MIT Press, 1962). Vygotsky analyzes the theories of the relationship of learning and development held by Piaget, William James, and the Gestaltists and then goes on to outline his own theory, the central feature of which is "the zone of proximal development." The interdependence of "scientific" and "spontaneous" concepts is exactly analogous to that of discursive and mythic forms of thought in Cassirer's philosophy of symbolic forms and Susanne K. Langer's philosophy of mind. The idea of development "upward" in spontaneous conceptualization and "downward" in the formation of scientific concepts is fundamental to Vygotsky's dialectical conception of learning and development as set forth in *Mind in Society: The Development of Higher Psychological Processes*, ed. Michael Cole, Vera John-Steiner, Sylvia Scribner, and Ellen Souberman (Cambridge, MA: Harvard University Press, 1978). See especially pp. 78–91.

4. See Prologue.

5. For excellent examples and interesting procedures, see Ira Shor, *Critical Teaching and Everyday Life* (Boston: South End Press, 1980), 155–94.

6. Susan Miller, "Rhetorical Maturity: Definition and Development," in *Reinventing the Rhetorical Tradition*, ed. Aviva Freedman and Ian Pringle (Conway, AK: L & S Books, 1980), 119–27.

7. I have learned a great deal from conversations with my friend and colleague Rosamond Rosenmeier, whose observation this is.

2

Recognition, Representation, and Revision

We should not be surprised that our students so often consider revision as a chance to get "it" right the second time around.[1] Despite recent attempts to differentiate editing and rewriting, most English teachers probably continue to instill the idea that revision is like taking another swing at the ball or shooting again for the basket. The idea of revision as correction is, like readability formulas and sentence combining, consonant with a view of language as, merely, a medium for the communication of our views of a reality *out there*: we have ideas and we put them into language. (Sometimes we might get the wrong slot: try again.) Language is often seen as a window which keeps us from enjoying an immediate vision. The pedagogical corollary is that the best we can do is to teach window washing, trying to keep the view of what is "really there" unobstructed by keeping the prose clean and clear. Revision, in this view, is polishing. I argue in the following that we can learn to teach revision as itself a way of composing if we consider it analogous to acts of mind whereby we make sense of the world.

One rainy afternoon last fall I stopped by to browse among some miscellaneous journals in the gaudy reading room of a

First published in *Journal of Basic Writing*, 3 (Fall–Winter, 1981). Reprinted in *A Sourcebook for Basic Writing Teachers*, ed. Theresa Enos (New York: Random House, 1987).

graduate school library where, as it turned out, I witnessed a basic writer at work. He sat in a low-slung, purple velour settee, a pad of lined paper on his knee, a nice new yellow pencil and a pack of cigarettes at the ready, and a Dixie Cup of coffee to hand. He seemed prepared for the labors of composition. He would write a sentence or two, light a cigarette, read what he had written, sip his coffee, extinguish the cigarette—and the two sentences. He had pretty much worn out the eraser by the time I left. (That would be an interesting research index: How long does the eraser last, if it is not bitten off in momentary despair?) My eyes glazed over more quickly than usual as I leafed through *Research in the Teaching of English* because my mind was otherwise engaged in formulating what I would have said to this earnest graduate student, if I had had the nerve. Something like this:

> You need to get some writing down on paper and to keep it there long enough so that you can give yourself the treat of rewriting. What you need is a ballpoint pen so you can't erase and some cheap paper so you can deliberately use a lot of it—and one very expensive sheet of creamy foolscap for your inventory of glosses: it's a sensuous pleasure to write on a beautiful surface after you've been scratching away on canary pads. But wait a minute! Where are your notes to yourself? Where are your lists? Where are your points of departure? Where are your leads? Where is your lexicon? Where are your quoted passages? Where is your chaos? Nothing comes of nothing! Here you are in this spaceship pod of a chair, this womb, with essentials like coffee and cigarettes, but without the essential essential —language! How can you know what you think until you hear what you say? see what you've written?

I think it is instructive to consider how the "writing behaviors" of this graduate student resemble those of our basic writers. There is, of course, a difference: whereas the graduate cannot get beyond the compulsive readjustment of the (doubtless) insubstantial and formless generalization he has begun with, our students hate even to start—for a dozen reasons which have been carefully formulated and studied in recent years— and once they do have something down, they are loath to touch it: those few words are hard-won and therefore precious, not to be tampered with. The graduate destroys by restatement because he does not know how to get the dialectic going; the undergraduate cannot conceive of adjustment or development because his fragile construct might collapse. But insofar as neither knows how to make language serve the active mind, they both are basic writers: they do not understand rewriting because they do not understand how writing gets written in the first place.

My tendentious claim is that the same is often true also of their teachers: revision is poorly taught, or is not taught at all, because composition teachers and composition textbook authors often do not know how writing gets written. Without a substantial understanding of composing as a dialectical process in which the *what* and the *how* continually inform one another—a nonlinear process motivated by both feedback and what I. A. Richards calls "feedforward"—there will be no way for teachers to differentiate between revision and editing, no way to teach revision not as a definite phase, a penultimate stage, but as a dimension of composing. Revision is, indeed, reseeing and it goes on continually in the composing process.

There is, of course, a great deal of talk currently about "the composing process," but there are very few pedagogies which are consonant with the kind of process composing actually is. I have elsewhere discussed the reasons for this state of affairs: current rhetorical theory has provided little guidance for our classroom practice because it has no philosophically sound way of accounting for how words work. There is no understanding in current rhetorical theory that in composing everything has to happen at once or it does not happen at all. If there is not something to think about, if there are not ideas to think *with*, if language is not in action, if the mind is not actively engaged, no meanings can be made. The pedagogical challenge is to help students take advantage of *allatonceness*, to see it as a resource, not the mother of dilemmas.

The linear sequence by which "the composing process" is commonly represented—prewriting, writing, rewriting—is antithetical to the "audit of meaning," I. A. Richards' term for dialectic. Instead of allatonceness, it suggests that there is a nonreversible order, a sequence of activities which unfold in a predetermined manner. The interrelationships of the triad are obscure; the notion, for instance, that pre and re have anything to do with one another, logically or psychologically, seems unheard of. If prewriting is, in many instances, presented as a matter of amassing the slottables, rewriting is considered a matter of checking out what has been slotted. "Think of what you want to say" in prewriting is matched by such instructions as these for rewriting: "Go back over what you have written. Are there any unnecessary words? Does everything you say refer to your thesis? Is your main point at the end of the paragraph? Are they any mechanical errors?" These questions are only transformations of the old imperatives: "Do not use unnecessary words. Assure that all statements support your thesis. Avoid mechanical errors." Get law and order. Plant a tree. Love your mother. People who have done a lot of writing themselves frequently consider it a self-evidently sensible thing to teach the use of this kind of checklist to inexperienced writers. What they leave out of account is that the experienced writer has criteria which are brought into play by asking such questions: that's what it means to have "experience."

I think it is fair to say that the linear model of composing as prewriting, writing, rewriting fosters a pedagogy of exhortation. Now, if we are to undertake to teach composing as a dialectical process of which revision is not a stage but a dimension, how can we prevent what was earlier described, the write—erase—write again—erase it all syndrome? The short answer is, as I have noted, to teach students to take advantage of the allatonceness of composing, to assure that they continually rediscover how forming, thinking, and writing can be simultaneous and correlative activities. Beginning writers need the experience of seeing how it is that consciousness of the *what* leads to understanding the *how*. This is what Paulo Freire means by "conscientization," the chief principle of his "pedagogy of knowing." If a pedagogy of knowing is to be the successor to the pedagogy of exhortation, we will need as models of knowing those acts of mind which are logically and psychologically analogous to writing, namely, perception and concept formation.

Taking perception as a model for writing lets us exploit the ancient wisdom that seeing and knowing are radically alike. Our word *idea* derives from the Greek *oida*, which meant both *I have seen* and *I know*. The eye is not a passive recorder; Ruskin's notion of "the innocent eye" has been superseded by that of "the intelligent eye."[2] When we see, we compose. Rudolf Arnheim lists as the operations involved in visual perception the following: "Active exploration, selection, grasping of essentials, simplification, abstraction, analysis and synthesis, completion, correction, comparison, problem-solving, as well as combining, separating, putting in context" (*Visual* 13). Is there any aspect of the composing process not represented in that list?

From Arnheim, E. H. Gombrich, R. L. Gregory, and other philosophers and scientists, we can learn that perception involves matching and reordering, from the molecular level on up: *Vision* is through and through a matter of *revision*. Indeed, seeing is actually contingent on reseeing. To clarify this fascinating fact, I have students read Owen Barfield's explanation of how it is that cognition depends on recognition. He asks the reader to suppose that

> he is standing in the midst of a normal and familiar environment . . . when suddenly he is deprived by some supernatural stroke of every vestige of memory—and not only of memory, but also of all those assimilated, forgotten experiences which comprise his power of recognition. He is asked to assume that, in spite of this, he still retains the full measure of his cognitive faculty as an adult. It will appear, I think, that for the first few moments his consciousness—if it can bear that name—will be deprived not merely of all thought, but even of all perception. It is not merely that he will be unable to realize that that square, red and white object is a "house" . . .; he will not even be able to see it *as* a square, red and white object (*Reclaiming* 39–40).

Seeing the point, my students speak of "Barfield's meaningless man." We can make meaning because we see in terms of what we have seen. Without remembered forms to see *with*, we would not see at all. Seeing is thus the primal analogizing in which thinking has its origin.

Now these philosophical principles of perception—seeing is knowing, seeing is contingent on reseeing, the intelligent eye forms by analogizing—provide the foundation for a pedagogy of knowing. How can we use what we can learn about perception in order to make observation not a preliminary exercise but a model of the composing process?

The allatonceness of composing is well represented by looking and writing in tandem. Since learning to record observations has a self-evident usefulness for everybody from nuclear physicists to nurses, from parents to doctors, and since observing our observations *requires* language, assignments which involve looking and looking again can rationally involve writing and writing again. Exercises which make recording and commenting correlative and virtually simultaneous have an authenticity which is unusual in composition assignments. One procedure which helps writers enact revision as a mode of composing is what I call a dialectical notebook: notes, lists, statements, critical responses, queries of all sorts are written on one side; notes on these notes, responses to these responses are written on the facing page. The inner dialogue which is thinking is thus represented as a dialectic, the beginning of thinking about thinking. This double-entry journal encourages a habit which is of immediate usefulness, since this format is the best there is for taking notes on lectures and reading. And it is easily adapted to what Dixie Goswami calls a "speculative draft," a procedure for writing papers which allows students to take advantage of allatonceness by keeping notes and queries, formulations and reformulations in continual dialogue on facing pages.

The dialectical notebook teaches the value of keeping things tentative. Without that sense, the allatonceness of composing is dangerous knowledge that can cause a severe case of writer's block. Unless students prove to themselves the usefulness of tentativeness, no amount of exhortation will persuade them to forego "closure," in the current jargon. The willingness to generate chaos; patience in testing a formulation against the record; careful comparing of proto-statements and half-statements, completed statements and restatements: these are all expressions of what Keats famously called "negative capability," the capacity to remain in doubt. The story is told of a professor of internal medicine who brought home to his students the value of this attitude in diagnosis with the slogan: "Don't just DO something: Stand there!"

Along with the value of tentativeness, practice in observation teaches the importance of perspective and context, which become ideas to think *with* as students practice observing natural objects, for instance, and observing their observations. A shell or pebble on the beach has one kind of appearance; if you bring it home, it has another. Such facts call for recognition, formulation, and articulation. In the practice of looking and looking again, of writing and writing again, as students learn to compare kinds of appearances, they are also learning that perception depends on presuppositions, remembrances, anticipations, purposes, and so on. In my own teaching, I hand out weeds and grasses, seeds and bones because natural forms are themselves compositions, pedagogically useful emblems of historical process. Friends and colleagues have occasionally argued that nature is an alien point of departure and that such an exercise as Ira Shor's examination of the contents of a wastebasket is more likely to engage the attention of basic writers. Detective work or archaeology is certainly as useful a metaphor for interpretation as nature study: the point is to make the transformation of the familiar to the strange and the strange to the familiar an exemplification of what goes on in all interpretation; to foreground the process of "reading," of construing, of making sense of whatever is under observation, from different perspectives, in different contexts.

Freire shows us how. The peasants in his culture circles, who are learning *how* they make meaning and *that* they make meaning simultaneously with learning to recognize words and sounds, study pictures depicting familiar scenes, reading them as texts, translating and interpreting them, and interpreting their interpretations in dialogue. What Freire calls "problematizing the existential situation" is a critical act of mind by which historical contexts for objects and pictures are developed: careful observation of what is depicted works together with the interpretation of its significance. Perception thus provides the point of departure for a pedagogy of knowing because it is through and through conceptual.

Problematic symbols and problem-posing pictures at one end; organic structures in the middle; at the other end, abstract designs and diagrams which we can ask students to observe, translating in the process from pictorial to verbal language. I. A. Richards, in a valuable essay called "Learning and Looking," suggests just how challenging that translation can be (*Design*). He is ostensibly discussing the problems of literacy training in societies in which depiction is not thought of as representational, but in the course of demonstrating how "reading" certain diagrams exercises the translation-transformation capacity necessary for handling the graphic code, he does much more. For one thing, he shows how comparing depends on the principle of opposition, which is essential to all critical inquiry into "what varies with what while the rest is treated as remaining constant." Even more important, he provides demonstrations of how perspective and context function heuristically. Careful looking and experimental translation teach the observer to use oppositions to limit the range of choices. Just as learning to keep things tentative is an all-important support structure for the concept of the allatonceness of composing, so learning the use of limits is essential if beginning writers are to understand that composing necessarily involves choosing. Limits are their means of defining and controlling choices; unless we teach the function of limits, no amount of exhortation will persuade our students to tolerate the risks which revision entails.

By keeping looking and writing together, we can teach revision as analogous to recognition in perception. If we can keep thinking and writing together, our students can learn how revision is analogous to the representation which language makes possible. Language has, of course, an indicative function, but it is its power to represent our interpretations of experience which is vital for a pedagogy of knowing. No thinking—no composing—could happen if we had no means of stabilizing images of what we have seen, of recalling them as forms to think about and to think *with*. Language is our means of *representing* images as forms: *forming* is our means of seeing relationships from one or another perspective and in different contexts.

Writing teachers have not, generally speaking, taken advantage of this power of language and mind—it was once called *imagination*—because linguistics, as institutionalized by current rhetorical theory, has no way of accounting for it. The conventional notion of thinking finds no room for the dialectic which language makes possible. It is based, rather, on the dichotomy of induction/deduction: either, it is thought, we go from "the data" to one or another principle, or we go from "high level abstractions" to the substantiating particulars. If teachers want to benefit from the fact that everything that happens when we think is analogous to what we do when we compose, they will need to form the concept of forming.

The logical ground for the analogy of thinking and writing is *forming*—seeing relationships, recognizing and representing them. Understanding that principle can show us how to start with thinking and writing together, and if we start with them together we will be more likely to keep them together. The way to bridge from so-called personal writing to so-called expository writing, from creative to critical writing, and, I will argue, from writing to rewriting is not to allow a separation in the first place. I want to concentrate now on one particular implication for classroom practice and course design of the premise that thinking and writing involve us in *seeing relationships*: how that can help us to teach revision not as a definite phase but as a dimension of the composing process.

From the idea that composing is a matter of seeing relationships, we might profitably conclude that at the pedagogical center of any composition course there should be not the grammatical unit of the sentence but the rhetorical unit of the paragraph.[3] Sentences depend on how they relate to other sentences; it is therefore easier to construe several sentences than it is one. The writer as reviser is a writer reading. Reading a paragraph, he has many points of entry; if he does not see a relationship as he starts to read, he might catch hold of another as he goes on. He can then reread and apprehend the earlier sentence. Because it articulates a structure of relationships, the paragraph provides a more appropriate focus for learning revision than the single sentence does. Apprehending the logical and rhetorical relationships of sentences in a paragraph is analogous to perception and concept formation in a way that apprehending those relationships articulated according to grammatical conventions *within* the sentence is not. That is why Gertrude Stein is right: "So paragraphing is a thing that anyone is enjoying and sentences are less fascinating."

Seeing relationships, as an idea to think with, can help offset the effects of certain theories of learning which, taking motor activity as the model, lead to the idea that because we must walk before we can run, we must therefore study sentences before paragraphs. Surely first things come first, but wherever language is concerned that will always mean that complexity comes before the allegedly simple. That is because meanings are not elements but relationships. It is by virtue of its complexity that the paragraph is simpler to take hold of than the sentence. This kind of paradox is central to the pedagogy of knowing. I do not mean that we ignore sentence structure when we teach revision. My point is that although errors are best identified in isolation, sentences are best revised in context, in the relational terms which the paragraph provides or which the would-be paragraph can be brought to the point of supplying. We are taking advantage of the allatonceness of making meaning when we teach our students to compose paragraphs in the course of revising sentences.

Along with the dialectical notebook, "glossing" paragraphs can raise consciousness of the interdependence of saying and intending. I ask students to summarize their paragraphs in oppositional form, to represent in a double phrase in the margin what is being set over against what. Thus identified, the logical structure of the paragraph can be used as an Archimedean point from which to survey the individual sentences. If it is impossible to formulate a gloss, that will tell a student more than exhortatory comments on incoherence ever could. Or it may be that in the process of glossing the student will express a hitherto unspoken intention which the paragraph can use. In that case, the gloss can be revised in sentence form and incorporated. Invention of needed sentences is contingent on recognizing the need; in my opinion, that recognition is inspired not by asking empty questions about what the audience needs to know but by seeing what the paragraph needs to say. To discover logical and rhetorical needs is to discover purpose, a process which is at once more complex and more manageable than trying to ascertain audience needs directly. They, of course, must be hypothesized and considered in conjunction, dialectically, with purposes. But to instruct the student to determine "the audience's needs" is frequently only an updated version of asking him to ask himself "What am I trying to say?" That is not, I think, a heuristically useful inquiry.

A way to encourage students to ask what a paragraph needs—what their argument or explanation or description or narrative needs—is to have them read their own paragraphs (a day or so after they have been written) a sentence at a time with the remaining sentences covered, anticipating at each period what the next sentence will be, will *do*, by writing one in its place. The writer can do this on his own, of course, but it is best done in conference or in company with other readers, dialogue being the best model of dialectic there is. The newly framed sentence can then be compared with the original sentence, of which it may, of course, be a replica: having two ways of saying to work with, or one way twice, is important in the practice of revision. The choice can be made, then, of which serves better in answering the perhaps newly felt need, but nothing should be thrown away, since the paragraph might well require the old original sentence in a new setting.

Developing a sense of rhetorical and logical form is in large part a matter of anticipating what comes next, of knowing what is needed, recognizing its emergence. That is not a "skill" but a power of mind, and it is exactly comparable to recognition in perception and representation with language. We do not need to teach this power, but we should assure that it is exercised. These simple techniques of paragraph review can serve that purpose because they keep the dialectic of intending and forming lively. Glossing and anticipating can help students see to it that the "what I mean" does not remain an amorphous, ghostly nonpresence but is embodied over and over again. To find out if you have said what you meant, you have to know what you mean and the way to determine that is to say "it" again.

Only when a paragraph has been reviewed in the light of its gloss, the various sentences abandoned or rewritten, restored, and reordered according to emerging criteria, is it time to work on sentence correction. Error identification is often tantamount to error correction and, as I have noted, that is best carried out if the sentence can be "heard" in isolation from its support system, the context which makes meaning rather than grammatical structure predominate. The procedure I recommend is to read the paragraph backwards aloud, sentence by sentence—an old proofreader's trick. If the student stumbles or hesitates, that is a sign of recognition and actual rewriting can begin. Nothing will come of this or any other such procedure, of course, if the student cannot recognize a faulty sentence when he hears one. By assuring that there are occasions for reading good prose closely, carefully, and frequently aloud, we can help our students to develop an "ear" for syntax, like an "ear" for music, to expect the way a sentence will go or can go so that when it goes awry, they can hear the error. The remedy for a deficient "ear" is hearing good prose, and that means that student writing will not be the exclusive "text" in a well-designed composition course.

When it is a simple matter of agreement, pronoun reference, tense consistency, or punctuation (in some cases), grammatical instruction can be useful. But sentences which fail because of pleonasm, faulty parallelism, misused idiom, or mixed constructions are, generally speaking, a different matter. They will yield to our grammatical analysis or the student's, but that analysis will serve no heuristic function.

Take, for instance, the following sentences:

The elemental beach and the music of the sea was more preferable than that other summer beach.
North Carolina is a state where the long straight roads

that lead to small quiet places has an unusually loud bunch
of inhabitants.
I have always seen that as a silver lining behind the cloud.
Teachers judge the quality of the student's performance
much like that of the farmer's grading his beef.

In my opinion, the best way to work with sentences like these
is for everybody in a small group, or for both student and tutor
in conference, to revise the sentence by means of composing
several interpretive paraphrases, using the parent paragraph as
a sounding board. Restating, representing is a way to recognize
intention: interpreting by means of paraphrase, rather than
tinkering with the incorrect sentence as it stands, allows a
student to call upon the resources he has for making meaning
which are independent of any explicit knowledge of grammatical laws. I do not mean that rhetorical and logical forms are
simply "generated": written discourse is not natural in the
way that speech, in a social setting, is. I have no faith that
well-formed intentions will surface from the deep if only gram-
marians will step aside. Returning to intention is a hard jour-
ney, but it is profitable because of what can be learned on the
way about the making of meaning.

Syntactical structures are linguistic forms which find conceptual forms: making them accessible to our students is one
of our chief duties. Kenneth Koch's experiments are important
to us all because they remind us of the value of teaching syntactical structures as generative forms rather than as slots to
be filled or inert elements to be combined. We can learn from
Koch and others how to make syntax itself a heuristic. The
procedure I have found most useful is called "persona paraphrase," in which a specific passage is selected, illustrating a
particular kind of structure. Students then copy its structure,
phrase by phrase, sentence by sentence, substituting completely different subject matter.[4] Kenneth Burke's conception
of recalcitrance explains the principle on which persona paraphrase is based: "A statement is an attitude rephrased in ac-
cordance with the strategy of revision made necessary by the
recalcitrance of the materials employed for embodying this
attitude" (*Permanence* 255). Insofar as it recognizes the dia-
lectics of recalcitrance, the paradox that complexity is simple,
the fact that concept formation is dynamic, the fact that saying
and intending inform one another—insofar as persona paraphrase is a technique which can teach revision as a mode of

composing, it is the antithesis of sentence combining. This is not surprising. It presupposes a philosophy of language entirely foreign to the conceptions which underlie the manipulations of sentence combining.

Revising at this level in these ways means slowing things down: allatonceness always does. Composing a persona paraphrase can take a full hour; composing interpretive paraphrases for a single conceptually faulty sentence can take up the entire class or conference time. It is time well spent, but there is a very difficult pedagogical challenge in seeing to it that this necessarily slow, deliberate pace is not the only one at which the composition course moves. Others have probably long since discovered the paradox I have been slow to come to, namely, that allatonceness requires a double track, if not a triple focus. Students should work independently on a long-term project for which the dialectical notebook is the enabling means of making meaning; they should continually be revising paragraphs with their fellow students; every day, in class or out, they should focus on the analysis and correction of a single sentence. The difference between the 101 section for basic writers, the non-credit course required of graduate students, and the Continuing Education workshops in writing should be a matter not of which elements are included but only of the ratios among them and the pace at which the entire course proceeds.

If we reject the linear model of composing and the pedagogy it legitimates—teaching the allegedly first things first; subskills before skills; the *know how* before the *know what*; walking (sentences) before running (paragraphs)—we will be free to invent courses which are consonant with the idea of the composing process as a continuum of forming. I have been claiming that recognition and representation, as the central operations of perception and concept formation, provide the models of forming which can help us teach revision as a way of composing.

Notes

1. This finding is reported by Susan V. Wall and Anthony R. Petrosky in "Freshman Writers and Revision: Results from a Survey," *Journal of Basic Writing*, 3 (Fall–Winter 1981).
2. Richard Coe brought my attention to the fascinating book with this title by R. L. Gregory. Coe's textbook, *Form and Substance*

(New York: Wiley, 1981), is one of the few which present perception as profoundly conceptual, as an act of mind as well as of brain.

3. I agree with those who argue that the paragraph is a rhetorical convention and that a single sentence may constitute a paragraph. See "The Logic and Rhetoric of Paragraphs," *Forming/ Thinking/ Writing* 215ff. For the time being, I use the term to mean a sentence sequence which displays logical coherence.

4. Phyllis Brooks, "Mimesis: Grammar and the Echoing Voice," *College English*, 35 (November 1973), 161–68. As Brooks notes, persona paraphrase is highly adaptable. I have described certain uses which my students have made of it in *Forming/ Thinking/ Writing* 211–15.

3

Abstraction as a
Speculative Instrument

Like imagination, meaning, representation, interpretation, intention, and form, abstraction is an idea we can't do without when it comes to thinking about the teaching of composition—which is to say, when we undertake to think about thinking. The fact that the first six do not commonly appear as terms in discussions of rhetorical theory and composition pedagogy is one measure of a significant failure in our profession, but the fact that *abstraction* appears continually is, unfortunately, not a sign of health. Abstraction is rarely well defined as a term and the complex concept it names is not generally well formed. For some, abstraction is a power of mind to be encouraged and trained; for others, it is a stylistic fault to be avoided. The fact that abstraction has a wide range of meanings is not in itself a danger; ambiguities, as Richards was fond of pointing out, are "the very hinges of thought." The trouble arises when the ambiguities are not recognized. In what follows, I will suggest reasons why abstraction is poorly understood and will try to show the effects of fundamental misconceptions of its linguistic and psychological character. I will also be concerned to define how abstraction might serve as a speculative instrument[1] in our study of composition.

From *The Territory of Language: Linguistics, Stylistics, and the Teaching of Composition*, ed. Donald A. McQuade (Carbondale, IL: Southern Illinois University Press, 1986).

For those who make the mind out of the senses—as Coleridge said of Locke—abstraction is the opposite of reality. Language, in this view, is unreal in itself, and the more abstract it is, the more unreal: as we move toward abstractions in our language, away from the particularities of space and time and the nameable details of sensory knowing, the farther we move from reality. When reality is posited as "out there," language is seen, logically enough, as a veil or barrier separating us from what is real, that is to say, the deliverances of our senses. In this perspective, abstraction is troublesome, considered the source of dangers to which we must be alert. The strong implication is that although we cannot get rid of abstraction, we should at least try to control its hazards by being "specific" and "clear." We may remember that Swift ridiculed the early proponents of the plain style in the figure of those academicians whose servants carried around sacks of objects which were deployed instead of words in their exchanges. Some modern theories of style entertain comparable suspicion of the abstractions that language makes possible, but distrust of abstraction in current rhetorical theory is more fundamentally an epistemological matter. It derives not from a rationalist rhetoric but from Bertrand Russell's logical atomism and the correspondence theory of truth. We meet it continually in the slogans and models of General Semantics, as popularized by Stuart Chase, S. I. Hayakawa, and James Moffett—the primacy of what is happening, the idea of language as a map for the territory of reality, the Ladder of Abstraction.

So regarded, in the linguistic perspective as it were, abstraction is, generally speaking, held to be hazardous. It is this conception teachers have in mind when they issue warnings *not* to "generalize." On the other hand, when abstraction is considered a "cognitive skill," it is equated with the capacity to generalize and is regarded as an important behavioral objective and a reliable index of intellectual achievement. It is this conception teachers have in mind when they ask "Where are your generalizations?" When *abstracting* is limited to *generalizing*, there is a strong need for other terms to name what has been left out: thus *poetic, expressive, personal, creative, affective, right-brain, nonlinear,* and *holistic* activities, behaviors, and operations are identified. There is no end to the attempt to address by lexical means the problem created by a logical and epistemological misconception.

Positivists conflate abstraction and generalization both as

acts of mind—or, as they say, "behaviors"—and as rhetorical strategies, because they do not recognize that abstraction proceeds in two modes; more accurately, they do not accept the idea of perception, artistic creation, and mythopoesis as being kinds of thinking which entail abstraction. The fact is—and it has long been established by studies of perception, by the analysis of dreams, and by the interpretive review of artistic creation—that we abstract not only by means of generalizing but also by means of what Susanne K. Langer calls "direct, intensive insight." Two formulations of hers can provide us with a working concept of abstraction:

> The perception of form . . . arises from the process of symbolization and the perception of form is abstraction (*Philosophical Sketches* 62).

> Abstraction is the recognition of a relational structure, or *form*, apart from the specific thing (or event, fact, image, etc.) in which it is exemplified (*Problems of Art* 162).

Symbolization, form, recognition, structure: all these concepts are needed for an understanding of abstraction as the fundamental act of mind. Symbolization keeps us from stretching abstraction to cover all responses to all stimuli, in which case its usefulness as a speculative instrument for the study of meaning is minimal. (Just so, if *communication* is stretched so that it includes the wiggles of sea anemones, it can't be of much use when we want to characterize the human use of signs.) The relation of abstraction to forming is also crucial, since it gives us the genus for a definition of abstraction. By identifying abstraction as the perception of form and the recognition of structure, we can thus proceed to differentiate "the ways recognition is achieved" (*Problems of Art* 163).

Abstracting by means of generalizing goes by many names, of which "reasoning" and "concept formation" are the commonest. Abstracting by means of apprehending gestalts—nondiscursively—is characteristic of what Cassirer calls "mythic ideation," in which parts stand for wholes, images bear conceptual significance, and spatial or temporal contiguity represents causality. Silvano Arieti's term for this mode of abstracting is "paleologic," in contradistinction to earlier practices of speaking of "pre-logical thought." Freud's "primary process," in which condensation and displacement remain undifferentiated, is another well-known name for the abstracting which shapes our dreams and the delusions of the insane.[2] The two kinds of abstracting are active and interactive in the mind, a reflection of the fact that whatever happens in one hemisphere of the brain is very complexly related to what happens in the other half. But the essential point is this: generalization requires abstraction, but we can have abstraction without generalization.[3] Abstraction seen as the recognition of form; as the symbolic representation of our recognitions; as enabling, but not requiring generalization—this is the conception of abstraction which can help us think about the composing process and composition dialectically.

Now, if we consider the Ladder of Abstraction in this light—as one of the chief models of the positivist understanding of the relationship of language and thought—it will be evident that it is incapable of representing abstraction in the nondiscursive mode. It is, in fact, a ladder of the degrees of generality, but that is not to say that it correctly or adequately represents the process of generalizing. (As I have noted elsewhere, only Buster Keaton could manage the Ladder of Abstraction dialectically.) Let us look carefully at these inadequacies.

Some of those who deploy the Ladder of Abstraction speak of moving *down* it as well as *up*, but the usual explanation is that students—everybody—should properly begin with particulars and move on up the rungs, always remembering that they are dangerously out of touch with reality, which is constituted by particular things.

Consider the Ladder of Abstraction in the light of Vygotsky's summary of his theory of concept formation: "When the process of concept formation is seen in all complexity, it appears as a *movement* of thought within the pyramid of concepts, constantly alternating between two directions, from the particular to the general, and from the general to the particular" (*Thought and Language* 80). The principle that simple particulars come first; that sensory knowing is a datum; that it is natural to move from particulars to specifics to "abstractions"—that principle is false. Perception is dependent on a primordial abstraction, as all cognition is on *re*cognition.

Consider the Ladder of Abstraction in the light of Rudolf Arnheim's recapitulation of his brilliant account of how the child apprehends visual forms:

The touch image of a surface, a shape, or an angle must be composed by the brain, just as it must create the visual image from a multitude of retinal stimulations. . . . The artificial distinction between perception and conception has been superseded by evidence that perception does not start from particulars, secondarily processed into abstractions by the intellect, but from generalities. "Triangularity" is a primary percept not a secondary concept. The distinction between individual triangles comes later, not earlier. Doggishness is perceived earlier than the particular character of any one dog (*Art and Visual Perception* 166–67).

The Ladder of Abstraction, by encouraging the identification of particularity with an unmediated sensory experience, misrepresents the dialectic of thought and feeling.

Consider the Ladder of Abstraction in the light of Ernst Cassirer's critique of the Realist epistemology it models:

Intellectual expression could not have developed through and out of sensuous expression if it had not originally been contained in it; if, as Herder said, sensuous designation did not already embrace a basic act of "reflection." The characteristic meaning of language is not contained in the opposition between the two extremes of the sensuous and the intellectual, because in all its achievements and in every particular phase of its progress, language shows itself to be at once a sensuous and an intellectual form of expression (*Essay on Man* 319).

The Ladder of Abstraction falsely models concept formation and it ignores abstraction in the nondiscursive mode, *viz.*, imagination, mythic ideation, primary process. It confuses abstraction with generality. It is entirely consonant with the idea that words name things without the mediation of an interpretant; it provides no way of representing context or perspective or purpose. The Ladder of Abstraction, insofar as it represents a philosophy of language and a theory of knowledge which can neither account *for* the process of making meaning nor give an account *of* meanings, should be abandoned in the interest of our learning to think *with* the concept of abstraction, to employ abstraction in all its complexity as a speculative instrument for the study of composition. Before turning to what it could help us explore, I want to consider the effect on research methodology and pedagogy of an unenlightened conception of abstraction as, simply, generalization and as the unproblematic antithesis of the concrete.

In a praiseworthy attempt to analyze the development of writing ability from high school into the later years of the university, Aviva Freedman and Ian Pringle aimed to measure intellectual growth, not just "rhetorical ability."[4] They wished to measure abstraction because it is "cognitive" and not just "rhetorical," explaining that they chose as "a potential index . . . the levels of abstracting, or rather the students' capacity for abstracting as revealed in the writing" (316). They carefully distinguish what they did from other attempts to measure abstracting capacity by focusing on T-units or by identifying as especially significant " 'statements at a high level of abstraction'," defined by some researchers as those which " 'propose principles or generalizations concerning life at large' " (317). They note their decision not to base their ratings on "abstractness of the diction or the abstractness of individual propositions" (317). Here, then, is the summary of their purpose:

> What we were interested in getting at in our analysis of these students' writing was not only the level of abstracting from experience that the essay was operating on, but also the degree to which the students had themselves formulated these abstractions. In other words, we wanted some measure of the number of rungs up the ladder of abstracting that the students themselves had climbed, as evidenced in their writing (318).

If formulating abstractions is what these researchers want to look at, how, one wonders, is that to be studied otherwise than in rhetorical terms? How is abstracting "evidenced" by writing if not in the language of the discourse—and isn't that what rhetoric is concerned with?

There are laudable statements throughout the article about the dangers of judging rhetorical skills as necessarily significant (unless, interestingly, they have *not* improved), but the only clue as to how one would go about judging the ascent up what they call the ladder of *abstracting* is said to be a "second-level classification"; in cases where a writer goes on to compare, say, authors and periods, that is, when he forms more general classes, that is said to be an even higher level of abstraction. "The student's capacity to abstract" is to be determined by how "the primary data" has been "classified, ordered, and integrated by the writer within some superordinate hierarchic conceptual pattern" (317). Apparently, they see classification, ordering, integration as matters not of "rhetoric" but of "cognitive process."

Freedman and Pringle display an ambivalent attitude toward rhetoric. They take as their own the conception of rhetoric which has been called, in an execrable instance of scientistic jargon, "the current-traditional paradigm." This ahistorical and wrongheaded identification of rhetoric with *bad* rhetoric accounts for their dismissal of "rhetoric" as unhelpful to them in their study of students' "capacities for abstracting"; nevertheless, they employ a "rhetorical instrument" to describe "the features of successful expository prose" (316). Rhetoric is identified with judging in terms of vividness, stylistic effectiveness, tone, and other such "mentalistic" criteria (where is "flavor"?); by contrast, intellectual processes, conceptualizing, creativity, generalizing, and, of course, "abstracting" are important to the measurement of cognition. By failing to articulate any relationship between "the cognitive aspects of the process" of writing and "the rhetorical features of the completed product," though they declare its existence (322), Freedman and Pringle do not recognize that they are dichotomizing what should be kept in dialectical relationship: they have given us another version of the positivist view of language as the garment of thought.

The dichotomy of rhetoric, which is considered suitable only for evaluating style, and abstracting, which serves as a measure of intellectual power, is analogous to the perennial dichotomy of the product and process. In both cases, failure to recognize and represent the dialectical character of the relationship is symptomatic of the failure to begin, as Vygotsky urged, with "the unit of meaning." Freedman and Pringle are committed to process; they understand its pedagogical importance and have taken as a point of departure in their research the sound principle that composition is properly evaluated only in the context of its creation and shaping. But apparently they think that by speaking of *abstracting* instead of *abstraction* they have made their allegiance clear and that nothing more is required. When they convert the Ladder of Abstraction to "the ladder of abstracting," the superficiality of this tactic is revealed, since the ladder in no way represents what Freedman and Pringle call "the heuristic power of the process" (314); in no way does it model that dynamic alternation which Vygotsky identifies as the essence of concept formation. In my view, unexamined assumptions and ill-formed concepts cannot be improved by tinkering with the models which represent them.

As an example of what I mean, let me note what happens in the discussion of "second-level classification": it is seen as less of an achievement than the formulation of those generalities reached at higher rungs of the Freedman and Pringle ladder of abstracting. But as we surely know—it is a self-evident fact and requires no research to be established—our students can name general classes very much more easily than they can specify. To rename a parsnip as a *vegetable* or an *ingredient* is a far surer sign of conceptualization in progress than renaming it *food* or *something you can buy at the grocery store*. Freedman and Pringle recognize this fact when it is considered as a matter of "rhetoric": they would not be taken in by big words or "generalizations about life at large," which they have wisely dismissed as unsound indices of intellectual power and command. But they apparently do not recognize that the same holds true when we are considering thought as a matter of "abstracting." It is their ladder of abstracting which traps them into considering that higher is better.

I believe that experimenting with ways of developing the rhetorical counterpart of concept formation is the research composition pedagogy most needs. I also believe that abstraction can serve us as a powerful speculative instrument when we come to consider the pragmatics of that relationship of language and thought. The questions I want to raise are these:

1. Josephine Miles has said that logic, rhetoric, and grammar provide ways of analyzing a writer's language, the means he uses to take him where he wants to go: What would happen if we analyzed and evaluated compositions, not in that split-level way which results from dichotomizing language and thought, product and process, rhetoric and cognition, but as a matter of interpreting symbolic expressions and representations of intentions?

2. I. A. Richards saw rhetoric as a study of "how words work": Could we approach student writing, looking for ways of relating how words work in relation to how concepts are being formed?

3. If we think with the concept of abstraction as the recognition of form, can we devise questions which would help us to determine if students are indeed forming concepts? Would they be like these?

- Has the student analyzed the question? Are the terms of the question/topic renamed, critically deployed? Is the question questioned?
- Is there any sign of a recognition of presuppositions? Are assumptions identified or examined? Are alternate perspectives or contexts considered?
- Do the transitions signal actual shifts or are they merely additive?
- If texts are cited, are they properly adduced? adequately explained? Is there evidence that the student can paraphrase in the interest of critical explanation?
- What about analogies: are there any? are they cogent? If there is an extended metaphor, is it logically developed?
- Are the specifics appropriate to the class names? Do the class names have the appropriate degree of generality?
- Are there any formal definitions? Are they logically sound, i.e., with both classification and differentiation? Are the examples characterized and evaluated? When conceptual terms are used, are they developed by means of *specific* names, i.e., intermediary between a high degree of generality and a low?
- Is there any attempt to develop an argument by means of the opposite case? borderline and model cases?
- What is the logic of error: are sentences faulty because of pleonasm and idiomatic snarls or because semantic requirements have not been met?
- Does the writer have a working lexicon for the definition of relationships, or are *enhance* and *contain* the all-purpose verbs, once *is* has been exhausted?
- Does the writer demonstrate an understanding of how to draw out the implications of an assertion or a description? Are concepts transformed to activities? titles to situations? events to a characterization of a state of affairs?
- Is there any sign that the writer has an understanding of the uses of style for the sake of articulation and emphasis? Are there any judicious repetitions? phrases in apposition? parallel structures?
- Has the semicolon been "dialectically" deployed?

The real challenge to pedagogy is to teach students how to make such questions their own. Students, using abstraction as a speculative instrument, can learn to draw on the resources of language itself in order to discover their intentions and articulate the relationships which thinking identifies. Thinking with the concept of abstraction as the recognition of form is a way to make thinking about thinking integral to the composing process; it is more likely, then, that students will learn to see revision as a dimension, not a stage, of the composing process. The current rage for revision, like the earlier "prewriting" fad, will have little salutary effect on composing practices if the underlying conception of language as muffin tins does not change.

Of course, abstraction as a speculative instrument can also guide *our* practice, both in the evaluation of writing and in designing the assignments which elicit what we get. The idea that abstraction is the recognition of form can help us speculate about how our students are forming concepts and sentences alike. Keeping abstraction-as-forming in mind can help us judge cogency of argument, as well as appropriateness of diction; soundness of definition, as well as control of syntax; the balance of particularization and generalization, as well as pacing of exposition. And because it can help us evaluate, abstraction as a speculative instrument can guide us in designing courses and assignments. In composing our courses in composition, what we most urgently need, I think, is an improved understanding of "development": abstraction, understood as the recognition of form, could help us speculate about what we are up to when we try to teach development. What would happen, for instance, to the notion of "supporting detail"? Consider the following; it comes from a text for teachers of writing:

> As an entity convenient to the creative effort for beginners, the topic sentence needs limiting right away from the start. Students need to state the topic of their paragraphs—and they need to state their opinions, reaction, attitude toward, or judgment about the topic there too. Thus a topic sentence that reads in a descriptive essay like 1 below is merely a statement of fact in which the writer proposes no generalization to support. Hence he runs into trouble in developing a point. In 2, however, there is a limitation and control right from the outset: 1. The room has black walls. 2. The room is dreary.

The doctrinaire assumption expressed here about the need for limits derives from the idea that generalizations are simply proposed—not formed, arrived at, but simply posited. If generalizations are not regarded as the result of forming concepts, then it follows that limits will not be seen as having any heuristic value; they will be seen simply as constraints. Instructing students to compose paragraphs by beginning with topic sentences and then "adding specificity and detail" (as this writer goes on to say) is certainly consonant with the idea that rhetoric is one thing and abstracting quite another. The speculative instrument of abstraction as forming focused on this misconception could help us reclaim what we probably know about the composing process, *viz.* that the way to substantiate generalization is not to limit (constrain) from the start but to amass particular observations from hypothetical points of view generated by a purpose, and to discover limits in the very process of ordering and balancing, specifying and classifying, describing and defining. The composing process *is* the process of forming concepts. Thinking with the concept of forming could save us from assigning a Descriptive Essay in the first place!

What is the relationship of fact to generalization implied in the passage quoted? A statement of fact is not the same thing as a proposition, nor does a statement of fact *propose* a generalization; statements of fact are one kind of support for generalization. Perhaps that is the point being made, but the implication seems to be, rather, that *in this case*, the statement of fact (sentence 1) proposes no generalization, whereas in sentence 2, *because* it is not a statement of fact, there *is* a generalization which can then be supported. But, of course, without context there is no way of knowing whether sentence 2 provides a very particular detail, a rather specific observation of a fact or feeling, or a tentative judgment, a generalization. The implicit dichotomies in this analysis of two topic sentences are fact/impression, objective/subjective, limitless/generalizable; they are illogical and unsupportable.

In an effort to forestall having students turn in an unstructured, pointless list, this textbook writer claims that only the expression of attitude has the power to elicit supporting details, since it is a generalization. The instruction guarantees, I would say, a paratactic lineup of impressionistic, adjective-ridden sentences. There is no reason whatever for expecting that the The-cat-is-on-the-mat predication of sentence 2 will necessarily encourage development any more certainly than would the recording in sentence 1 of a surely extraordinary fact, that the room has black walls! There is plenty implicit in that image: think of it as nondiscursive abstraction and see what you can find. Encourage students to think with that image, and generalizations will be drawn out, developed. Generating a "chaos" of names in response to *walls* and *black* will yield not just synonyms (though they can be useful) but meanings—and meanings become the means of making further meaning. Inviting students to compose sentences, then, from and with these words is to assure that the dialectic will get started, that concepts will be formed, because it is the nature of syntax to bring thought along. Making the heuristic powers of language accessible to students is the surest way to teach them how to move from abstraction in the nondiscursive mode to abstraction in the discursive mode. The best way to get the dialectic going is to get the sentence going; the easiest way to do that is to convert assertions, statements of fact, expressions of opinion to "iffy" questions—the strategy C. S. Peirce called *abduction* and Paulo Freire calls *problematizing: If the walls are black . . .*

Abstraction in service as a speculative instrument could help protect us against the "gangster theories" (I. A. Richards' phrase) represented in the disquisition on topic sentences I have cited and in other such wrongheaded instruction. Thinking with the concept of abstraction as forming could certainly reveal the inadequacy of seeing development as a matter of getting the right topic sentence and adding on the allegedly "supportive details." But I want to make the further claim that abstraction-as-forming can help us keep meaning in focus by defining the commonalities of abstracting and rhetoric, of language and thought. And this is surely what we must do if we are to make the case that writing is a mode of learning and a way of knowing.

In my view, the real usefulness of abstraction as a speculative instrument will become dramatically apparent as we undertake the definition of the role of writing in the arts and sciences. That is because it can show us how to think of forming concepts as a matter of composing. I am convinced that our colleagues will not be attracted by the maundering banalities of reading specialists, the abstruse treatises of psycholinguists, the question-begging models of cognitive psychologists (whose understanding of language is generally no less primitive than that of the behaviorists), or the intellectual shallowness of most rhetoricians; and if they are contented at first with the quick answers some composition specialists give them to their naive questions ("How can I teach writing *and* cover all the material in my course?"), they will soon be back, sometimes merely irritated, but often with a new consciousness of the complexities of thinking about thinking. It is at this point that abstraction can clarify Richards' claim that "all studies are language studies, concerned with the speculative instruments they employ."

Collegiality is fostered in those concerted efforts which typically follow in the second and third phases of instituting programs in "writing across the curriculum." We might be surprised to find that we have something to learn, especially from scientists. In discussions of writing in the disciplines, it is generally assumed that it is the job of the invading rhetoricians to teach the historians and the biologists and the anthropologists. And so it is: we must certainly work hard to demonstrate that writing is not editing and we will of course want to show how writing can function as a mode of learning. But once we have engaged our colleagues in this enterprise of teaching writing as a composing process, we should open our minds to the fact that we have something to learn from teachers in other disciplines when it comes to thinking about thinking. For one thing, we could quickly discover that the aim of a context-free description of something happening in the immediate environment based on observation whose purpose it is to gather "data" is recognized by working scientists as an illusion. They write up their experiments in a way that suggests a controlled single-mindedness, but the actual process is quite different. Like writing, scientific research is a composing process—full of accident, confusion, contradiction, befuddlement, as well as the temptation to smooth out what is fundamentally complex and to ignore the genuinely problematic. It will be easier for us to persuade our colleagues that writing is both a creative and a critical activity of forming if we develop the argument to discover that that is, precisely, how best to define the search for evidence, the presentation of cases, the preparation and execution of experimentation, the articulation of interpretation.

We will discover in thinking with our colleagues about writing and the teaching of writing that we are engaged in a philosophical enterprise. J. Robert Oppenheimer, a scientist

and a teacher for whom thinking about thinking was a pleasure
as well as a professional duty, had this to say:

> Science is a search for regularity and order in those do-
> mains of experience which have proved accessible to it. I
> am not sure that the effect of the impressive victory of
> man's mind in this enterprise has not been to make us a
> little obtuse about the role of the contingent and partic-
> ular in life. It is true that many particulars can be under-
> stood and subsumed by a general order. But it is probably
> no less a great truth that elements of abstractly irrecon-
> cilable general orders can be subsumed by a particular.
> And this notion might be more useful to our friends who
> study man and his life than an insistence on following
> the lines which in natural science have been so over-
> whelmingly successful (*The Open Mind* 24).

It has been my aim here to suggest that abstraction employed
as a speculative instrument can help us rethink the nature of
the relationship of "the contingent and the particular" to "the
general orders."

Notes

1. The phrase is I. A. Richards': "All studies are language studies,
   concerned with the speculative instruments they employ" (*Speculative Instruments* [New York: Harcourt, 1955], 115–16). I have
   discussed this phrase and the understanding of mediation it implies
   in several places: "I. A. Richards," in *Traditions of Inquiry,* ed.
   John C. Brereton (New York: Oxford University Press, 1985); "I. A.
   Richards and the Audit of Meaning," *New Literary History,* 13
   (Fall, 1982), 63–79; "Speculative Instruments," in *The Making of
   Meaning* 113–26.
2. For a succinct explanation of "mythic ideation," see Ernst Cassirer,
   Language and Myth (New York: Harper, 1946). Silvano Arieti explains "paleologic" in *Creativity: The Magic Synthesis* (New York:
   Basic Books, 1976). Freud explains "primary process" in *The Interpretation of Dreams.* The most important non-discursive form
   is art. Since verbal art is *discourse,* there is a terminological problem; recognized and solved, I think, by introducing the word *vir-
   tual.* See *Feeling and Form* (New York: Scribner's, 1953).
       The chief reason for avoiding the terms "conscious" and
   "unconscious" as names for the two kinds of abstraction I mean
   to differentiate is that depending on them forestalls the attempt
   to understand how consciousness and symbolization are "simul-

taneous and correlative," as Owen Barfield puts it. We need, I think, to make all phases of composing conscious in this sense; we need to teach ways to *represent* developing intuitions and intentions and to differentiate that process of consciousness from *self-consciousness*.

3. Coleridge makes this fundamental point in the fifth of his Philosophical Lectures.

4. In "Writing in the College Years," *CCC*, 31 (October 1980), 311–24.

II

Is Learning Still Possible?

Yes—if we remember that it is by interpreting our interpretations that we make the meanings which will serve as the
means for making further meaning.

*　　*　　*

Students do not need to learn to interpret nor do they
need to learn how to interpret their interpretations: they are
born interpreters. But they must discover *that* this is so. We
should offer them assisted invitations to discover *what* they
are doing and thereby *how* to do it. Relating the *that*, the *what*,
and the *how*, each to the others, is a dialectical, recursive,
critical, and creative process which spirals on toward a pedagogy of knowing. It is empowered by "the sense of learning."
The teacher's principal role is, I think, to provide opportunities for students to discover that interpreting is what they're
doing when and as they make sense of the world. The model
for interpreting is perception—or so it becomes, once we have
reclaimed imagination as the forming power of the mind. Triadicity as a speculative instrument helps us discover that we
never just *see*; we always *see as*. The capacity to *see as* is the
source of the power of analogy, which empowers all thought,
in whatever mode. To *see as* is to re-cognize: thinking begins
here, with recognition. It requires, then, that we stabilize our
recognitions so that we may remember them, return to them,
consider them anew. Language provides the means of representing our recognitions and thus of interpreting our interpretations. That activity is "the sense of learning."

4

Is Learning Still
Possible?

I think it's probably true that I learned half of what I may claim to know about teaching composition in the first two weeks I spent in a classroom forty years ago. In no time at all, I concluded that a theoretical knowledge of grammatical rules bore no necessary relationship to a capacity for writing sound sentences and coherent paragraphs and that students who couldn't read carefully were poor writers. I discovered that I. A. Richards was right—that if everybody understood what you meant right away, you'd have taught nobody anything; that he was right, too, about pedagogy and mountain climbing—if people don't feel the tension of the rope, they feel insecure. I learned that neither corrections keyed to the handbook I was required to use nor lengthy comments I was proud to be able to concoct effected any improvement; that things went best when echoes and analogues became apparent. I certainly knew from my own experience in both a newspaper office and graduate school that compositions did not grow from outlines. Nothing unsettled my belief that ideas develop when they are felt to have a significance beyond the context in which they first appear. But the other half of what I think I know about teaching people to write was hard-won.

Published as "From Dialogue to Discourse to Dialogue," in *Reclaiming the Classroom*, eds. Dixie Goswami and Peter Stillman (Portsmouth, NH: Boynton/Cook, 1986).

Some twenty years later, after teaching composition to some of the best students in the country, I took a position at an urban university where my students bore little resemblance to those at Bryn Mawr, Haverford, and Swarthmore (or so I thought), and I discovered that I didn't know how to teach them: I didn't know enough and what I did know didn't seem to help. Learning what I needed to know and reclaiming what I did know has not always been an exhilarating experience, but it has been immensely interesting. It required inventing new procedures (new for me) for discovering what was actually going on in my classroom. To interpret those findings, I turned to philosophy. For one thing, pedagogy is unspeakably boring unless it is conceived in philosophical terms, but the real point is that unless practice is guided by theory it will indeed be aimless and teachers will be increasingly desperate. I sought philosophical guidance to bring theory to bear on practice and to let practice correct theory. What follows is an account of how I came to see the classroom as a philosophic laboratory.

After the first discouraging month at UMass/Boston, I decided that unless I could get people to talk, there was not going to be any learning. But how was I ever to do that, to elicit any response from the bewildered people who faced me in sullen rows? The answer came from a student, the first young man I'd ever seen with shoulder-length hair. In conference I asked him who he was and how he came to be at UMass, since he was clearly not in the mold of my other students. He was from Maryland and the only member of his class not to go to Princeton or Bard. He'd come to UMass because he wanted to be in "the real world." "Why don't these real people talk?" I asked him. "Because," he said, "they've never had a teacher who asked questions she didn't know the answer to. It scares them! And they are contemptuous of you when you demonstrate that you're thinking things out as you talk, that you don't already have the answer." I knew he was don't already have the answer." I knew he was right and asked him to help me by talking up in class. He promised he would.

Now, I was dedicated to the principles of the New Criticism and I wanted everybody to have the text in front of them. We were reading *Leaves of Grass* in a beautifully printed version of the first edition, but it had begun to occur to me that the text-and-I was not the model to follow if I wanted conversation to develop, so the first class meeting after my conference with Jonathan the hippy, I wrote the following line from *Leaves of Grass* on the board:

Who goes there? hankering, gross, mystical, nude. . . .

"Okay, please form two groups. Turn your chairs so that you more or less face one another across this midline. Now I want you to talk to one another, to people in the other group, about that line."

When the noise of chair-arranging subsided, there was a dead silence. Realizing that I was not going to be able to resist posing questions, I took off my scarf and tied it around my mouth. A few embarrassed giggles and then silence ensued. Suddenly Jonathan said, "I don't see why *mystical* is in there." Instantly, there was a response: "Well, *that* doesn't bother me! Of *course* he's mystical! He's mystical all the time! But why does he say it's *gross*?" Another comment, instantly: "He doesn't say IT's gross. He means he *feels* gross." "Well, wouldn't *you* feel gross if you took your clothes off in the woods?" "No . . . well, I don't know, but maybe he thinks somebody *else* would think so." They were talking! They were even thinking! I can't remember what followed and, because I hadn't yet learned to log my classes, I have no record to return to, but I will never forget that first time hearing my students talk with one another about a shared text, making sense out of it in the exchange of responses. I reclaimed that morning the knowledge that dialectic and dialogue are consonant and cognate, simultaneous and correlative.

I came to value this kind of exchange however it can be encouraged, whenever it develops, as a sign that the dialogue with the text, which is the point of departure for all critical reading, is being REpresented in a social context and has thus become accessible to critical response and review. I decided that the final paper in this freshman course should somehow involve dialogue, so I asked my students to interview someone over forty (this was 1968) about life in America before World War II. Consternation! "I don't know anybody that old except my parents, and I sure can't talk to them!" "Try it," I said. "They will want to talk about this and you might find what they have to say rather interesting." The one stipulation was that the paper could not be in dialogue form. They could write in the first person or they could transform their notes into a short story; they could write an essay.

Even before I got the papers, I was pretty sure that something interesting was going on from what I overheard in conversations they were having with one another. When the papers came in, I was astonished. They were lively and touching, amusing and full of wonderful stories and scenes and moments, all emblematic of American life in the Great Depression. More than one paper included a postscript noting that the student had never before understood what his parents meant in talking about how things were different in those days—about the change in values. So not only had they learned how narrative and "telling detail" and voice all worked to REpresent feelings and judgments: they also had found it possible to talk to their parents, to listen, and learn. I was proud of having invented this assignment; I had never heard of Studs Terkel or sociolinguistics or oral history. I can remember meeting Lewis Mumford at a party and telling him about it. He congratulated me on doing something about bridging the generation gap, which was the topic of the day.

In subsequent years, I continued the search for ways to get the dialectic going and, as it has turned out, all these heuristics have been analogous to dialogue. As a shorthand term, I call them *oppositions*: they are all ways of REpresenting the inner dialogue, which is the mind in action as we see relationships. What I call an "opposition" is any relationship—spatial, temporal, causal. The simplest, most flexible, most powerfully generative opposition is a line drawn down the middle of the page. In this instance, the idea came from thinking what I could do in conference that would teach composing, not editing. I had decided that conference time was too valuable to be spent on explaining this or that error, that it would be more profitable if I could offer a method, a procedure, something for students to do which might possibly forestall their committing some of the errors in the first place. Most errors result (as Ken Macrorie shortly made abundantly clear) from a mismatch of intention and wherewithal: there was often no purpose, and that emptiness was being camouflaged by tricking out insubstantial assertions in half-remembered conventional expressions, cant phrases, clichés, and periphrastic clouds. I admit that for a time I was so disheartened by the fragments and fractures of "basic writing" that I was tempted to see "Engfish" as a step in the right direction, but I soon found that it was absurd to clear away the thicket to let the undergrowth flourish: there *was* no undergrowth, no healthy stock which needed only the light of rhetorical encouragement! I concluded that teaching writing was better modeled by careful work in the greenhouse and the cold frame than by breaking sod, draining swamps, or irrigating deserts. Engfish was not worth the time it took to correct it; the real solution was to see to it that students didn't write it in the first place.

In conference one afternoon, when I hadn't been able to elicit a single statement about a *tree*, I took a blank piece of paper and (probably) with a degree of exasperation drew a line down the middle, writing TREE on one side and then (probably) shouted at this inert young man to tell me what trees *do*, what they're *for*. And he started naming what trees do and what they're for: *they grow; they look good; they're for shade; they're for building with; you can hang swings and people from them.* "Look what you've done!" I (probably) shouted. "You've got half a dozen sentences!" He saw simultaneously that there were no sentences and that out of what he had set down in those columns he could *make* sentences. The line down the middle of the page taught him—and me—that predication is sometimes easier to generate schematically than syntactically.

I took this idea to class, asking students to categorize the sixty or so words we had listed in the course of going around the room three times recording responses to a photograph of a rice paddy from Steichen's *Family of Man*. What two words from the list could serve to name categories in which we could group the remaining fifty-eight? I then asked that everybody compose a poem in Whitman's manner. (I had again chosen *Leaves of Grass*.) The list provided the lexicon and the category heads, the conceptual armature; we had by then discussed the principal characteristics of Whitman's style. The inert young man wrote a poem which I can't quote, because I had not yet developed the habit of copying significant student papers, but I remember that after a nicely organized catalogue of observations made by the poet as he stood watching the activities of the rice paddy, he ended with this line:

At dusk, I go home refreshed.

I thought then that perhaps he'd learned how to think with the oppositions of *them* and *me*, *here* and *there*, *beginnings* and *ends*, *dawn* and *dusk*.

*   *   *

The following year, my friend and colleague Rosamond Rosemeier suggested that she and I should design a course, to be taught in two sections, called Report Writing, in which we would try to teach what you need to do to write a good report, but to do so *not* by reading or writing "reports" but by recording the close reading of poems and stories carried on in something called "small groups." There were several Jonathans in the class and I made them my allies in a version of "each one teach one." They were responsible for some memorable breakthroughs, as when one of them brought a Vietnam veteran to a new understanding of Sarah Orne Jewett's characters in *The Country of the Pointed Firs*. The veteran had scoffed at "these elderly Shirley Temples," but this young black man gave him an *ex tempore* lecture on how Elmiry Todd, the herb gatherer, is a shaman, an exemplar of that figure in any community who represents spirit and power. But on the whole, I found the unit of the small group almost as inappropriate for the composition class as that of individual readers, each in communion with his own text.

It was this frustration with trying to teach via small groups that led to the first, deliberate attempt to report to myself what in the world was happening as my class suffered atomization. These logs allowed me to explore the shape and form of the exchanges in these small groups. With the help of an excellent tutor assigned to my section, Jean Parsons, I began to see that whenever students recognized how to use the limits of the readings to their advantage, they wrote in a more purposeful and focused way.

In order to "foreground" those limits so that the thinking they elicited could be REpresented more directly in their writing, I radically changed my reading list. Whereas I had normally assigned one or two novels (*Bread and Wine, Man's Fate*), three or four poems and a tract (*Pacem in Terris*), I began preparing several short passages on a single theme, favoring the unit of the paragraph. I assured that they were tough—hard to read, recalcitrant, perplexing—so that I wouldn't need to plead with the class to spend an hour reading a single page. And I assured that the ideas set forth would seem, once in hand, to have deserved the hard work required to apprehend them. I juxtaposed passages from works by Kierkegaard, John Donne, and D. H. Lawrence, for instance, and asked students to decide which two seemed clearly to have something in common which could then be set over against the third selection. To make this manageable, I taught them to gloss the paragraphs, a procedure (described at length in *Forming/Thinking/Writing*) which they could follow in order to formulate their understanding of the conceptual armature on which the paragraph had been shaped. The fact that their individually composed glosses could very well differ helped teach the essential dialectic of perspective and context. Whatever struck them as important as they paired paragraphs and set them in opposition to a third was *their* discovery; it wasn't an inert thesis statement prepared according to a sentence pattern offered like a muffin tin, nor was it a matter of finding a topic sentence, waiting like an Easter egg to be uncovered.

This experience convinced me that small groups are effective only when they return the student to a text—not necessarily his own—for the purpose of interpreting interpretations. And this is not a matter of opinion swapping; I share the impatience many teachers feel about what they often call "relativism." We do not teach that opinions are subject to correction simply by eliciting many different ones: opinions are interpretations and must themselves be interpreted. Interpreting interpretation means conducting an "audit of meaning" (I. A. Richards' definition of dialectic) in order to see how changing words changes meaning and how intentions can be reshaped as language REpresents them. I have argued in *The Making of Meaning* that the chief pedagogical value of encouraging an awareness that there can be, logically, no final answer when it comes to interpretation is that it encourages students to make careful arguments to support their interpretations. And this is not a matter of debate; as Richards notes, "the disputant is commonly too busy making his points to see what they are" (*Speculative Instruments* 50). The debate is only the mirror image of the rap group—which is often the actual form of "peer group" exchanges—so far as their nonheuristic character is concerned: neither fosters the dialectical exploration of meaning.

I was ready, then, in 1974, to compose a composition course dialectically, letting the exercises and assignments grow from one another, encouraging a spiraling by which we could continually return to the fundamental acts of mind which are in operation at all times as we make sense of the world. I began with the premise that composing is what the mind does. My point of departure was the idea that whenever we respond critically to what we see, we apprehend form; forming, thinking, and writing are thus consonant with one another and whatever can be learned about one will strengthen the others.

The armature for *Forming/Thinking/Writing* was provided by a newly devised course offered by the Department of English in recognition of the fact that our freshman English sections were not doing the job we wanted them to do and indeed that no two-semester sequence would be adequate for the majority of our students. The principles were clearly in mind. First, Intermediate Composition would not confuse composing and editing, but it would offer assistance in editing; we would work hard at learning ways to identify and correct syntactical errors. Second, there would be room for experimental and "creative" writing insofar as they could serve heuristically to enlighten the students about the nature of composing. Third, we wanted students to think about thinking, to develop a method of composing which would stand them in good stead in other courses.

I wanted them to see how they could learn to use in writing whatever they already knew about how to make sense of the world. During the first week, I brought in bits and pieces collected from several workbenches, dressing tables, and kitchen drawers and asked that each student choose something from the array of junk and, observing carefully, write a description which could then be developed as a definition. My shocked discovery was that nobody knew the definition of a definition, much less how to go about formulating one. We established that definition requires the naming of a class but that classification is not enough; definition requires differentiation of one member from others of the same class. ("A table is a piece of furniture" classifies without defining.) The idea of context came instantly into play when we tried to "define" a perfume bottle. If you juxtaposed it to an oil drum, it was clearly a *container*; if you considered its shape, it was just as clearly a member of the class *decorative piece of junk*. I soon saw that definition is concept formation in miniature: the class name was neither the point of departure nor the inevitable end; it emerged from the dialectic of particularizing and generalizing. I learned, too, how the process of defining made dramatically clear the need to question in order to generate names—identifications and generalizations—with which to compose. From logging those questions, I learned another way of teaching the uses of chaos.

From one student, we all learned how definitions grow

out of understanding function, which careful observation guided by judicious questioning can identify. This young woman was a ship carpenter and she knew what was what:

> A stove bolt is the only kind of bolt that is used without a washer under the head and unlike all other bolts when recessed into wood, it looks like a screw rather than a bolt.

Uneconomical and awkward, ready for editing, but full of *telling* detail, the kind required by definition. *Stovebolt* thus became emblematic of the naming of particulars from which generalizations could be developed to arrive at class names. (Somebody suggested that successful pieces of writing could be published in a weekly newsletter called *The Stovebolt*. Some years later I returned to that idea, and in Advanced Composition, I always begin with the Sentence of the Day, either a splendid bit of syntactical deployment or a tangled mass of fractured idiom.) I sent everybody to the dictionary to study the shape of lexical definitions and we experimented day after day in class with generating a chaos of names on the board which could then yield *genus* and *differentiae*. We came to see naming as *implicit classification* and classifying as *organized comparing*.

John Wilson's *Thinking with Concepts* (1963), a little book written for British high school students and often found useful in graduate seminars in this country, helped us develop our definitions when it came to abstract concepts. Particularizing and generalizing work together in all thinking, but it is harder to get the dialectic going when the point of departure is a general term. (For that reason, assigning topics is an antipedagogy if we want to teach the composing process.) Wilson suggests that after conceptual questions are separated from those of fact and value, a procedure which is somewhat more problematic than this linguistic philosopher lets on, the next step in critical analysis should be to lay out an argument by means of developing the model case and contrary, related, and borderline cases—in that order. Pedagogically, it is not an appropriate response sequence because it is not psychologically, or epistemologically, sound. (The same misconception is at work when Wilson admonishes his readers not to begin writing until they know what to say!) That is to say, thinking of counterexamples and logical opposites is much easier than determining right off the bat what an idea IS: the model case is what the writer wants to develop; it can't so easily be his point of departure, unless we are teaching composition as a set of conventions. Setting topics—which were once called common places—yields, precisely, *commonplaces.*

Developing cases—moving from contrary to borderline to related to model cases—was an excellent way for the class to learn how the logical analysis of ideas is comparable to observation and continual questioning in the case of stove bolts and oil valves and nutmeg graters: *What is it for? How does it work? What does it remind you of?* are all questions as appropriate to an understanding of a concept as they are to the description and definition of strange and familiar objects.

Another continually useful way of starting the dialectic of concept formation was Kenneth Burke's notion of thinking of names as titles for situations. It is a real advance to learn to move from *What is it?* to *What is happening? What has happened? What could happen?* Photographs—mostly of figures in a landscape—served as points of departure in practicing transformation as a way of generating new contexts and perspectives. The heuristic value of "reading" images—of interpreting scenes as if they were texts, of converting texts to scenes—came clear when one student, on her own in another course, used a photograph of Bogotá as a point of departure in composing a paper on a modern city. She saw the photograph as an emblem of the kind of place it is. This idea of pictures as spatial representations of events or processes, of something ongoing, led to using natural objects in an advanced composition course the following year. Shells and pods and burrs are symbolic indicators of process: they point beyond themselves to other times (past and future), emblems of their own history.

It was essential that class discussion be structured so that the dialectic of dialogue could be apprehended. If the first problem I encountered at UMass was silence, an equally trying one was confused babble. The trick was to encourage a certain direction without seeming to squelch others—and yet squelching is part of composing, of knowing when and how to choose amongst promising lines. I saw my job as that of a conductor who could say, "There! What have you done with that point? What does it suggest? How do you know?" Looking and looking again was matched by saying and saying again. This kind of return provides the best practice a writer can have for the central activity writing entails, which is revision. It is, of course, the very antithesis of the merely repetitive which drill depends on.

Rereading too—reading and reading again—came to be seen as the way to learn to interpret, to learn to paraphrase as a mode of critical reading. Students were mystified by this procedure, which was once at the heart of the teaching of reading. I think paraphrase has an especially important role to play, now that foreign language study has virtually disappeared from the school curriculum. A comment of one student brought me to see how to explain it: "You seem to be satisfied with paraphrase: Is that what you mean by *interpretation?*" Well, yes and no: interpretative paraphrase involves more than lexical substitution; it involves asking, "How does it change the meaning if I put it this way?" I don't know of any activity of greater importance for a writer to practice than changing words and observing the consequent shifts in his meaning. It is not a "skill" to be developed like a capacity for diving or place kicking. Writing as revision means learning to see meanings as dependent on how you use words in responding to your emergent interpretations. Reading in this way is indispensable in the composition classroom, if we want to teach the principle that how we construct is how we construe. When we compose, we do what we do when we read: we interpret what we are saying and hearing.

Looking and looking again; saying and saying it again; reading and reading-and-writing it again, watching the "it" change. And listening: the fact that listening, like reading, requires a lively expectation of what might be coming next is what makes it such good practice for the writer; all language use requires the sense of developing, emerging meaning. I read a short story aloud and had the class take notes as if it has been a formal lecture. Katherine Mansfield's "Miss Brill" served very well since the point of view holds steady; the descriptions and metaphors are continued throughout the story; it has as neat a shape as a sonata or a formal dance. When I described what I wanted them to do, there was consternation: "But how do we know what to listen for?!" I didn't stop to point out that the question is analogous to "I don't know what to say!" and "I don't know what to write!" but noted in my log that the question arose from the anxiety caused by years and years of being asked, "What is the author trying to say?"—a favorite of English teachers and not so much a generator as a suffocator. I suggested that they should listen for repetitions; that they

should imagine the scene described as a kind of frame which
is going to determine the pattern. I read and they listened and
noted; they then wrote for ten minutes in response to the question "What does Miss Brill learn?" The question is analogous
to "How does it look if you turn it around?" Several were able
to understand *learn* as a concept that had to be formed, to see
that it entailed *change* and that my question was a heuristic.
But I learned in the discussions that followed just how little
they'd been taught about how to read/listen. Years of symbol
chasing had not taught them such general principles as, for
instance, the consonance of season with action (or, of course,
the ironic dissonance of seasonal imagery and theme). If an
"old maid" is described as sitting by herself in a park in the
autumn fantasizing about the theatricality of the lively scene,
certain limits have been established, certain structures have
been sketched so that images and juxtapositions can be expected, and, as it were, *recognized* when they appear.

I decided that my students could learn to take better notes,
that they could train themselves in patterns of recognition, if
they could develop a procedure which would allow expectation
and recognition to work together dialectically. It occurred to me
that law students take notes on paper ruled with wide margins;
as they review their lecture notes, they annotate by listing
relevant cases and other references. Two columns, one played
over against the other, could encourage the idea of generalizing
tentatively while the lecture or reading was in progress and
could help make notetaking a *dimension* of listening, not something else that somehow had to go on concurrently with listening. Teaching them how to take notes by letting the double
entry represent the dialectic helped my students discover that
listening is interpreting and that notes can record the progress
of their meaning making.

The following year, I worked out a sequence for my writing assignments, the logic of which was based not on topics,
raw or refined, but on that constant movement of thought from
generalization to particularization and back which Vygotsky
defines as the dynamic of concept formation. I tried to keep
this complexity in every assignment as a way of teaching the
allatonceness of composition. The greatest challenge was to
find an order in which each exercise, as it echoed and reflected
previous ones, would be seen as "a partially parallel task," as
I. A. Richards puts it. Something learned from any one of them

would thus be useful and appropriate for the others. Borrowing a phrase from Richards, I called these exercises "assisted invitations" to students to find out what they were doing and *thereby* how to do it. Indeed, I wanted to call the emerging textbook *Assisted Invitations*, but a friend who's a librarian observed that it might be catalogued with Emily Post. Since the assignments invited students to think about what they were doing in writing; to discover the power of an active mind in forming concepts; to reclaim their imagination in this process of composing, I decided to call the book, instead, *Forming/ Thinking/Writing: The Composing Imagination.*

5

Skill, Skills, and Subskills

Recently, I spent two days talking with schoolteachers at the annual convention of the California Association of Teachers and another two days conferring with research scientists at the Cell Biology Lab of the University of California, Berkeley. An interesting juxtaposition. That year at the Lab there were two visitors from Britain, and I was interested to see that they did not have the composition problems which plagued the Americans. Both British and American scientists find it difficult to move from the mile-high pile of data to the Nobel Prize-winning paper, but at the sentence level and in composing paragraphs, the British scientists simply do not write awkwardly or unintelligibly. On the way to the airport, I asked my friend, Mary K. Healy of the Bay Area Writing Project, if she had an explanation for this difference. Just what would account for the fact that the British did not write like C— sophomores? Her answer was quick. The British, she said, *on the whole*, consider reading and writing as normal, natural activities which are expected to go on all the time in school and out. They do not depend on basal readers and they do not refer to the "Language Arts." I would like to consider here why it is that we Americans are less likely to consider reading and writing as natural and normal.

Versions of this chapter have been delivered at conferences at National Writing Project sites coast-to-coast.

74

For a working definition of learning I turn to one of the three psychologists I trust, Gordon Allport: "Learning—whatever else it might be—is surely a disposition to form structures." Learning seen as a disposition to form structures and an understanding of limits as enabling: why aren't these ideas guiding our practice? A "disposition" to form structures sounds natural: if it's natural for human beings to form and choose within limits, what's keeping us from teaching so that our students, K–35, are actively engaged in forming and making choices? I think it's because teachers and those who train, direct, and control teachers are under pressure to be "practical"—and *forming* sounds "theoretical." Practical people often are suspicious of theory: if practice is practical, they reason, theory must be impractical. Of course, they are themselves guided by theory, only they don't call it theory: they call it *research findings* or *political facts* or *common sense* or *The Real World*. And the theory which is killing progressive education before it's ever been tried, as Edward Steinberg puts it —the theory which is in the driver's seat, so to speak—is one which considers philosophical perspectives completely irrelevant. To entertain ideas in a philosophical perspective, you have to ask what they mean and that isn't a national pastime just now. Current theory encourages talking about "excellence," on the one hand, and basic skills on the other. I will discuss certain attitudes toward skills before turning to a consideration of how we might reclaim the idea of learning as a disposition to form structures.

The word *skills* is, of course, highly problematic. A little etymology can help in such instances, not because words should mean what they originally meant but because the history of a word's changing meanings can tell us about those meanings. In the seventeenth century—and before—*skill* was used principally of our Creator. When Marvell describes Lord Fairfax's kitchen garden as a second paradise, he tells us that God has provided another Eden:

How well the skillful gardner drew
Of herbs and flow'rs this Dial new.

And in the early nineteenth century—at least in Kentucky— skill belonged to the schoolmaster, not to his students. I know because I have my great-great-grandfather's contracts in which it is stipulated that the aforementioned John Anderson "doth agree and oblige himself to teach the undernamed subscribers' children to the best of his skill and judgment and the children's capacity." That was in Madison County, Kentucky, in 1814. Two years later, in Barren County, the contract has a different wording which is full of implications. Old Johnny had decided to be more specific in the matter of payment and he has listed the equivalent prices for the commodities which he is willing to accept in payment: flax at 25 cent per lb.; pork at $3.25 per hundredweight; corn at $1.20 per barrel, etc. There are other details of interest to the social historian, such as the fact that the rates and terms of payment have also been changed, but whatever happened in Madison County, John Anderson must have decided that it was a bad scene. He moved on and continued until he came to Iowa, which is where he died in 1848. What I find most interesting in comparing the two contracts is that in the second one, mention of "the children's capacity" has been omitted. Maybe he thought that if he stipulated *that*, he'd have no students at all! In any case, reference to the schoolmaster's "skill and judgment" remains.

Now if we jump 170 years, we find—do we not?—that *skill* is imputed not to teachers but to students. I don't remember any job description in which the *teacher's* skill is mentioned. Furthermore, *skill* has now become *skills*: the plural form overrides and I will return to this point in a moment, but for the time being, here are some anecdotes about skills.

The first concerns the mechanization of skills and it's called "Nuns and Computers." The story comes from Susan Andrien, who is one of the teachers I count on to keep me honest. While she was in my seminar at UMass, she was teaching in one of the so-called "magnet schools" in Boston, a school to which had been allotted special resources so that students would be drawn to it, thus helping the process of integration. The Boston School Committee thought that the special resource was a computer program called System 80 because 80 percent of students answer correctly 80 percent of the questions 80 percent of the time. System 80 is a million-dollar machine and program in which "human information processing" is factored into fifty—count 'em—skills. They include where to put the comma in direct quotations and *organization*. The machine has an electronically coded voice; and what the kids generally heard was "NO-o-o-o-o: try again! NO-o-o-o-o: try again!" One morning Susan heard a terrific racket in the computer room and when she went in to check she found a student pulling out the wires and pounding the delicate buttons and shouting "YOU try again, you——! *You* try again!"

The School Committee, I say, was under the impression that the special resource in that magnet school was System 80, but in fact it was Susan Andrien. She developed a course along lines suggested by Paulo Freire's "generative words," a course in which students problematized the imagery of television advertisements and wrote their analyses. There were no unexcused cuts allowed and the writing was continual: the kids lined up for that course. Susan did a lot of teaching in conference and one day when she was working with a student, another one asked for help and Susan said, "I'll be with you in a minute. You go work with System 80 until I'm ready." Now you should realize that students drawn to the magnet school often came from parochial schools—and this little girl was one of them. After a minute or two, she was back. Susan said, "Didn't I tell you to go work with System 80?" and the little girl answered belligerently in her Dorchester accent: "I went ovuh theah, but Sistuh Matey ain't theah!" This student showed a laudable resistance to the idea that a machine could teach her . . . though I am aware that some computerized programs are more interactive, more dialectical than some nuns.

The appeal of factoring skills into subskills is so powerful that it can befog the vision of teachers who know better. One group of teachers in a first-rate suburban school system undertook to prepare a manual which would help everybody teach The Basic Skills. But its real purpose was to protect teachers from parental attack. On PTA night, in response to anxious or hostile questions about Sean's or Sandra's basic skills, the teacher could reach in the file drawer and retrieve a manila folder in which graphs were to be found showing progress in the development of, say, comma-using skill. Of course, on these graphs the line generally went up, but ascending or descending, the significance of those lines was political, not pedagogical: those lines said "BECAUSE we are measuring what is learned, we teachers know what we're doing!" Meanwhile, the teachers who compiled this manual added an appendix in which they observed a disconcerting fact: "We should note," they stated, "that there seems to be no correlation between the development of single skills and the skill of writing. Students who have dramatically improved their subskills may not write any better and those whose charts indicate no progress in the development of subskills may nevertheless write acceptable reports and essays."

We should not chide the teachers for not chucking the manual. It is very hard to admit that a two-years' investment of time and energy has been profitless. My guess is that these teachers have by now set aside the manual of teaching basic skills and have returned to the idea of *skill*—in the singular—and its relationship to judgment. Those who factor skill into skills and skills into basic skills and basic skills into subskills are convinced, I suppose, that by isolating particulars they can teach the whole.

Factoring skills into subskills and then sequencing those skills leads to the idea that sequencing is itself a skill. And of course it is, if you take skill with judgment to mean *knowing how* by *knowing what*, but that is not generally what is meant by *sequencing*. A teacher in a recent seminar told us of having to administer a test to her students—middle-aged women, mostly black, preparing for the high school equivalency diploma. The purpose of this test was to determine the reasoning capacity of these women and it concerned the steps you go through in changing the oil filter in the engine of a car. Dorothy Nelson described how these women puzzled over what they read, trying to sort out what in the world they were being asked to do and getting very angry—to the point of throwing everything into the wastebasket. What would have happened to the assessment of these women's cognitive skills if they'd been tested about something with which they'd had some experience? *And what does experience mean here?* It doesn't mean purpose or interest or intuitive understanding. Experience means, in this case, having some imagery to think with; knowing what an oil filter looks like would surely help in understanding questions about the sequence of steps in changing it. Experience means having a vocabulary of pertinent terms; it means for one thing knowing what a *filter* is—any kind of filter: what it *does*. Experience means being able to develop analogies on which our classification capacity depends. If we can't tell what something is *like*, we won't be able to tell what *kind* of thing it is. Human beings don't just see; we can't just *see*: we must *see as*. We must see *in terms of, in the light of, with respect to*: that's the price we pay for being human beings, for being language animals, or, if you prefer, it's what the Fall of Man means. Human experience is mediated by symbolic processes. We human beings, even

PhDs, can make meaning only if we have the means and those means are meanings—metaphoric, schematic, analogic. These women were being asked to make sense of a sequence *without* the means of forming the concept of the kind of sequence in question. When Dorothy pointed this out to her so-called superior, that woman said, "But they *must* learn to pass this test! Sequencing skills are very important!"

Dorothy wisely did not attempt to explain the problematics of sequencing the tasks entailed in learning to sequence. She set about assuring that her students could find the means whereby they could make further meaning. She undertook to develop what I. A. Richards calls *comparison fields (Reclaiming* 176), some experiences which would enable her students to form the concept of sequencing. A comparison field is what you draw on in order to *see as* more clearly; to be able to say *that reminds me . . . it's a little like . . . it's very different from . . . if you look at it this way, you can see . . .* etc. Dorothy had read Shirley Brice Heath on "Doin' Ethnography" so she invited one of the English Department secretaries who is a Penobscot Indian to visit her class. Nicky talked about her family, her tribe, her nation; about continuity and heritage; about language. She told of taking her grandson to meet the patriarch up in northern Maine. There's nothing like a little oral history to help students see how a comparison field can be developed. Her students began rediscovering their own history, their own lives, their own powers. She then took them to the Museum of Science to visit an exhibition of Chinese arts and crafts, presented there in historical terms, in a continuum with an antique loom in operation next to a contemporary embroiderer. Her students began to be able to think of themselves *in terms of . . . with respect to . . . in the light of . . .*: all these phrases signal comparison fields, the possibility of *seeing as* in different ways. Sequencing, like outlining, is a very late stage in thinking and composing. Sequencing is not taught by assigning the identification of sequenced steps. *What comes before what*: knowing that entails knowing how to question and interpret the tentative answer. It can be taught only by having students learn to form the concept of sequence—and that requires a working knowledge, an experience with different kinds of sequences: logical, rhetorical, numerical, narrative.

Maybe we could call that "From oil filters to comparison fields," but in any case this story is meant to represent the problems created by reducing *skill* to *skills* and failing, then, to relate those skills to *judgment*. *Skill* means knowing *how* by knowing *what*. It means finding the *how* by means of exploring and analyzing the *what*. Johnny Anderson kept skill and judgment together because he knew, I think, that learning how to do something comes from knowing what you are trying to do. How you teach—your practice—comes from knowing what you think you are doing. Teaching, I. A. Richards counseled, is a matter of offering students "assisted invitations to discover what they are doing and thereby how to do it."

If we could develop the concepts signaled by *thereby*, I think we could take advantage of what I like to call allatonceness. The single most important fact about forming significant (meaningful) structures, about making meaning, about reading and writing, is that everything happens at once or it doesn't happen at all. We make meaning, we discover what we want to say as we name and rename, as we relate and represent the relationships we discover. All this recognition goes on all the time. The really interesting challenge is to make this allatonceness a resource. That means teaching the uses of chaos, learning to tolerate ambiguity while finding the ways out of chaos. None of this activity is linear and it cannot be dichotomized.

Allatonceness is a very powerful concept: indeed, it is the only theory I know that's powerful enough to protect us from what I call the Killer Dichotomies—ones like The Affective Domain and The Cognitive Domain; creative writing and critical writing; left brain/right brain. Most studies of hemispheric dominance have been carried out on subjects whose brains have been surgically cut in half. Normally, the two halves of the cortex are joined by a structure called the *corpus callosum* through which a steady stream of impulses travels over millions of fibre tracts. (The Corpus Callosum Society, which Jean Pumphrey, Jean Sanborn, Virginia Draper, and I founded, is dedicated to an appreciation of the relationship of the two elements of *any* dichotomy.)

In my view, one way to take advantage of allatonceness is to stop isolating creative and critical thinking from each other, to stop designing courses in which expository prose is the meat and potatoes and expressive writing is Dream Whip. Or, indeed, to teach courses in which argumentation and exposition have been abandoned. I teach artists to draw inferences and I teach scientists to develop metaphors, not because I want to give the artist a chance to be critical and the scientist a chance to be creative, but because both inference and metaphor are at once critical and creative. Both are means of making meaning; both are means of abstracting; both are means of expressing and representing. Metaphor and inference are both forms which find other forms: unless we see what they have in common, it will be very difficult to understand how they differ, the kind of limits they offer us, the kinds of choices each enables.

Here's what happens when we forget that all acts of mind and all modes of discourse entail forming structures. I have a pair of anecdotes and then I will return to allatonceness.

The first is called "Sean and the Windmills." A young friend of mine had an assignment in junior high which went like this: "Write a research paper on something that interests you. Find out what you need to know in the library and write four or five pages." Now Sean understands machinery and has direct, personal knowledge of windmills, so he chose them for his subject. He investigated several kinds, made drawings, interviewed owners. He went to the library to check the facts. He composed a paper which was both sound and delightful— in the opinion of his mother. Sean's paper got a B— and this comment: "You have only two references; there were supposed to be five." You can see what happened: The teacher thought she'd cleverly planted one foot in each of the domains of the affective-cognitive dichotomy. By letting the children write about what interested them, she'd covered the affective front; by having them go to the library, she'd covered the cognitive. The fact that interviews constitute a kind of documentation and that field study is relevant to understanding escaped her.

That is an anti-right-wing anecdote, if you follow me: it reveals the faults of rigid taxonomies which value what is alleged to be critical over the allegedly creative. But there is just as much trouble being made over on the left. A good example of left-wing dichotomizing is provided by recent research in which something called the "natural purposes" of writing are extolled and set over against what is scornfully called "displaying information." But "displaying information" is not necessarily the antithesis of the "natural communicative functions" of language. Does the terminal on the travel agent's desk serve an *unnatural* function? Isn't it *natural* to want to know when your plane will arrive in Tucson? It is wrongheaded to identify the display of information exclusively with stultifying workbook exercises and with having students simply give back what they've been given. The *natural* functions of language include representation and communication. It is folly to forget that fact.

These researchers are frowning on a function of writing which is extremely important and extremely interesting, especially to youngsters. To illustrate the truth of that assertion, let me tell you about Andrew Crossley's Bears. When Andy was six, he was fascinated with animals. His mother told me of how he'd made a poster featuring a whale and the slogan "Save the Whales!" He'd propped it up in the driveway in the hope of discussing this problem with interested passersby. He was quite annoyed when an old lady patted his head, saying "What a pretty *fish!*" I asked Andy's mother to describe his writing procedures; here's her account:

> The following is typical of the pieces Andy prepares at home, usually on his typewriter. Sometimes he calls them "certificates" and sells them to us, even signs us up as subscribers for the coming year. Thus he supplements his allowance. He has absorbed the phrasing of the Golden Guides and other such books and can now reproduce it on his own. I'm particularly fond of this one because it incorporates a reference to something that really happened . . . to Bob.

Thus Andrew Crossley:

> Black bears. They range from California to Massachusetts. They are the commonest bear in all North America even though my father saw a brown bear in the Blue Mountains. Its favorite food is wild berrys but it will eat small mammals fish and plants. 6ft. height to 8ft. height. In the winter it builds a den under fallen log or rocky ledge. In late winter two cubs are born. Its South American relative the spectaled bear isn't as big as a black bear.

I think we can say that Andy was experiencing what it feels to be a writer: he was pretending to be a naturalist and he was pretending to write like a naturalist. So far as he's concerned, displaying information is, without question, in the Affective Domain. Andy is intent on making meaning, and he has chosen his limits carefully and respectfully, but it would surely be absurd to instruct him to edit out the reference to his father in the interest of making the genre pure. There will be plenty of time for consistency later on—and later on, he will know all about Blurred Genres.

I think we should proceed with the assumption that reading and writing *of all sorts* are natural activities, well within children's capacities. Otherwise, we are defenseless against basal readers and the idea that the way to teach writing is to factor it into subskills and minitasks. The best thing that could happen in composition pedagogy would be for the whole notion of assigning topics to be abandoned. As it is, the needs of the testing industry must be met, apparently, by assigning topics. Here, for instance, is the summary of a report on research on writing assignments:

> Researchers have been working on a model of the composition assignment which sets forth fifteen dimensions of a writing assignment: instruction, stimulus, cognitive demand, purpose, role, audience, content, discourse, specification, tone and style, preparation, length, time, number of drafts, and criteria for evaluation.

The categories, the report concludes, are intended to give test makers and teachers a set of tools for "adjusting" writing *topics*! Test designers who labor to identify fifteen dimensions of the task of setting topics are, of course, the same people who brought us System 80. People who think of *cognitive demands* in the same terms as they think of *style* and *stimulus* are the ones who put *comma use* and *organization* in the same sequence! Apparently, it never occurs to them that unless and until students invent, develop, and formulate their own topics, they will not be learning the chief thing in learning anything, namely, how to ask "WHAT am I doing and HOW can I do it?"

Many people seem to think that learning to write means, simply, having something interesting to write about and that it is thus the teacher's prime duty to offer topics. One of the bestselling NCTE publications is something called *What Can I Write About? 7,000 Topics for High School Students*—for example, what to do about skunks under the porch. You can see the positivist mind at work: motivation is to be found in the *content*, what positivists love to call The Real World; kids will be interested only in something itself interesting; therefore the challenge is to find Interesting Things to write about, Interesting Topics. The premise is false: nobody learns to write unless his or her mind is engaged and the mind is not engaged by *things*, no matter how interesting, but by forming structures. Learning is not possible unless and until there is forming activity.

That activity means the active mind making meaning in a community of four-year-olds or sixty-four-year-olds—amongst people for whom it is important that we say it this way, not that way; important that we see it as this or that; important that we tell it like it is or the way we see it. *Active learning* suggests to us that students should find, invent, develop their own topics! Basic skills, I have been suggesting, grow from the habit of exercising skill and judgment together, all at once; from the practice of making meaning by deliberately reflecting on the means of making meaning. Behavioral models of language activity are mischievous: learning to read and write is NOT like riding a bike; thinking about what you're doing in that case is likely to make you fall off the bike. But making meaning requires reflecting on what we are doing and it's from that thinking about the *what* that we will get the *how*. The activity of the mind is essential to authentic learning. Richards believed this so deeply that he suggested that we pronounce *activity* in a way which would make it special: he suggested a Scots accent and he spelled the word with a double *e* (*acteevity*) so that we would have to stop and consider what we mean in order to learn how we might foster it. Motivation, he declared, comes from the mind's acteevity, from the *doing*: "It is the lure of the task itself, not some adventitious jollying up."

Instead of searching for topics, we should exercise our skill and judgment in assuring that minds are engaged so that the children's capacity is properly exercised. Our writing assignments should have that as their aim. They should indeed be *sequenced*, each building upon what has gone before so that students will recognize "the partially parallel task," to call once more on I. A. Richards' way of putting things. And each assignment will prepare for what's to follow. I think it's useful to think of those parallels in two dimensions: up and down and side by side. That is to say, each assignment should have a place in a sequence and there should be several sequences going on at once. When students get the habit of writing away at several projects in different stages all at once, it is more likely that minds will be engaged; that students will be continually forming structures and will therefore be learning; that they will be inventing, questioning, discovering, and formulating and thereby deciding on their own topics: they may even decide to write about what to do about skunks under the porch.

6

Images of Allatonceness

In composing, everything happens at once or it doesn't happen at all. We don't think somehow wordlessly and then put our thoughts into language. We speak and seek for meaning at one and the same time. The only way to teach the composing process, I think, is to apprehend the dialectic of language and thought by beginning with "the unit of meaning," as Vygotsky argued. To teach the composing process entails coming to terms with allatonceness, learning to consider it not as a source of roadblocks but as a resource. When we write, we are simultaneously naming, inferring, referring, recognizing, remembering, marking time, wondering, wandering, envisaging, matching, discarding, checking, inventing: all at once, we are carrying out these acts of mind as we are writing something down—or up —making meaning in the process. The challenge, as I say, is to take advantage of that allatonceness, not to fractionate, reducing composition to skills and subskills. We need to teach ourselves and our students to manage the complexity of allatonceness, to learn to tolerate uncertainty and ambiguity, to recognize the value of *not* knowing what your thesis statement is and thus discovering the uses of chaos.

A talk given at the conference organized by the UCI Writing Project, the San Diego Area Writing Project, and Boynton/Cook Publishers at the University of California, Irvine, and San Diego, December 1984.

For teachers of composition, the principal challenge is to understand writing as a process, but unless and until we develop sound, substantial ideas about what *kind* of process composing is, we won't know how to alert ourselves to the possibly fraudulent claims of those medicine men who want to sell us the patent medicine which they promise will cure all deficiencies. I agree with I. A. Richards, who wrote that the main function of a theory is to protect us from "gangster theories." Research in the field of composition and rhetoric produces one gangster theory after another.

When educational theorists come to explaining the composing process, they almost inevitably break it down into components, elements, bits and pieces, which they then line up again in stage models. Of course, proceeding in a linear fashion is entirely appropriate when plowing a field or performing a ceremony or doing the wash or carrying out any other task in which some things *must* come before others, in which sequences are regulated or, as we say nowadays, "rule-governed." But when we move from any such process to learning something new, to any act of making meaning, to symbol making of any kind, these linear models will not serve. In planning a picnic, for instance, you'll find that a linear model, if adhered to strictly, will very likely kill the spirit and spoil the fun. That's because picnics are contingent social acts, not ceremonies or mechanical operations. Some things have temporal and logical priority: if you don't leave the house by 9:00, you'll never find a parking place at the beach. But it is surely tiresome to be in the hands of a picnic master who decrees that the olives and celery must be eaten NOW, regardless of the fact that a game of catch is nicely under way or a shell-collecting expedition has been organized.

It is disheartening to see how the idea of process is presented in textbooks as being constituted by rule-governed procedures. There is an active resistance to apprehending the real character of the composing process because doing so would change everything we do: to teach composing as the kind of process it really is would upset us: it would transform, it would revolutionize our practice. Many teachers do not want that kind of change and they will do anything to forestall it. They therefore tack on to whatever they are doing an inert, unexamined idea of the composing process. And what are most of them doing? Assigning topics and evaluating products. It is unimaginable to most teachers that writing can be anything other than thinking what you want to say on an assigned topic; that teaching is anything other than thinking up what students are to write about. The energy which should be going into forming the concept of composing as a process of making meaning goes instead to inventing topics, as cute or as compelling as possible—what to do about skunks under the porch or who is to get the kidney machine. They crave procedures which will get them off the hook, will let them get through the week's paper load without thinking about what they are reading and why it has been written. What they want is a way to teach writing pretty much the way the Maytag does the wash. If the idea of the composing process helps line up the tasks so that a five-paragraph theme emerges, what else could anybody want? And what's wrong with washability as a model for readability anyway? I once heard a voice coming out of a conference room at the 4 C's, as I walked down one of those Kafka-like, spirit-killing corridors—a voice saying, "It doesn't matter why it works! Theory is beside the point! It's like an oven: you want to be able to put in the casserole, set the dials, and take it out at a certain time—and it doesn't matter how the stove works!" This desperate problem solver didn't want to think because the only way she could imagine handling the paper load was *not* to think about it. And of course, as she probably teaches it, the writing she gets is driving her crazy! What I find difficult to understand is not the desire to keep from thinking about what you're reading in such circumstances, but the reluctance to see that terrible writing—or dull "good" writing—is the artifact of bad assignments. If Engfish is what we get, Engfish is probably what we deserve.

I claim that the idea of the composing process is useful to us only when we let it guide us in changing what we are doing, transforming our practice so that we can in fact teach composing as a process of making meaning. And if allatonceness is the chief characteristic of the kind of process composing is, then we will need ways of representing that idea to ourselves and our students.

The representation of theory is a problem that interests me a great deal. May I quote myself on this? In explaining the format of *The Making of Meaning*, which has as a subtitle *Metaphors, Models, and Maxims for Writing Teachers*, I have written as follows:

How can we make method out of theory? How can it guide our practice? Theory must be accessible; it must be there when we need it, or we will find that our theoretical interest wanes and, with it, the intellectual energy needed for teaching composition. In my opinion, the best way to keep theory lively and practice responsive is to have *in mind* models and metaphors to *remind* us and our students of what is involved in learning and teaching the composing process.

Making meaning is not properly modeled by motor behavior because although it of course entails motor behavior, it is essentially symbolic activity. Now, having asserted this incontrovertible fact, let me qualify by saying that any activity can help us imagine the allatonceness of the composing process, if we see it with the eye of imagination. Let me speak from my experience as a profoundly unathletic person. I am radically deficient when it comes to eye-hand coordination and I have no idea of where my feet are. A few years ago, a friend of mine offered to teach me to ski cross-country style. There was no mockery in her pedagogy, but it was heartless. No sympathy was offered, though she was tolerant of repeated error—and I am completely capable of going counterclockwise when asked to turn clockwise, etc. Her instruction was to do thus and so with my knees, to hold my arms this way and not that way, etc. All that happened was that I continually pitched forward and fell in the snow. But suddenly across the meadows, I saw a figure going like the wind—a young man in shorts and a tee shirt, obviously a serious skier! And as I watched I suddenly saw the whole shape of the act of skiing; I saw the Gestalt; I got the rhythm, the allatonceness of the action. I did what I saw and I shot across the snow! What I had needed was not a *model* which could show me how the various gestures and stances and operations fitted together, but an *image* of how cross-country skiing *looks*, and kinesthetically, how it *feels*. The image of the skier gave me the whole process; it represented the allatonceness of cross-country skiing.

I have suggested as a model of the composing process the double helix of the DNA molecule. Wherever it is cut, the double helix reveals the structure of the whole: the basic relationships are represented at every turn of the spiral. The framing structure of the helix represents those acts of mind which are ongoing, present in every phase of composing; I call them *naming, opposing, defining* (*Forming/Thinking/Writing* 61–109).

But for all its usefulness, the double helix does not tell us what composing feels like. My friend and colleague, Alice Trillin, who has produced three films for use in teaching writing, has noted that her aim was "to give students the experience of what it feels like to be a writer." The double helix can't do that: it spirals away as serenely as a barber pole—but there is nothing serene about the composing process. We could turn the helix into a spiral staircase and think of running up and down it—looking down on where we've been, on the turns we've built upon, running back down. But though that is the very antithesis of serenity, it does seem reckless and perhaps futile. I offer therefore another image which suggests the energy and purposefulness of the composing process without a hint of linearity: as an image of composing, I offer that most recursive of recursive creatures, the Border collie at work.

The shepherd knows that he must keep the Cheviots separate from the Black Face since he doesn't want any cross-breeding of his pure stock. A fence takes care of that problem, which otherwise would require a herd of sheepdogs perennially at work, and quite a few shepherds. The shepherd's dog works with him whenever he wants to relocate his sheep. He needs, let us say, to move the newly shorn Cheviots to new pastures. Let me describe the process as I once observed it in the Hebrides. The sheep were to be driven to the high pastures below the basaltic cliffs—up a very steep grade. The sheepdog was directed by Duncan's cries and whistles. There were some Gaelic words, but most commands were in International Shepherd Code: "Hi!" "Schweeee-bye!" "Ho! Ho!" I watched as the collie raced back and forth, nipping at the shorn flanks when necessary, moving the herd diagonally up the brae. He seemed to have no trouble at all, dashing down the road to redirect a few malingerers, sly or obtuse; doubling back to assure that others didn't break free on the far side. And with every third dash or so, he would charge down to the little compound where I was standing to urge a single ewe and her lamb to join the others —or so I thought. When all the sheep were in the upper meadow, Duncan closed a gate and started back to the farm. As he came by, I asked him why the dog hadn't been able to get the ewe and the lamb to join the others. "Och!" said Duncan, "I want them kept down here! The big one has a hurt foot and she couldn't manage up there; she might abandon the wee lamb.

The dog separated her and kept her down here, where I can keep an eye on her."

Well, I'm not going to allegorize and make the ewe and the lamb the introductory paragraph and its thesis statement, but I do think that the dialectic of shepherd and sheepdog is a nice analogy of the relationship of intention and saying, and I think that the sorting and gathering, the hithering and thithering of the collie in order to assure the general direction of the flock is representative of the activity of composing. When I asked Duncan if he'd trained the dog himself, he said "I have. But there's a good bit that's intuitive." That's true, too: we have to learn to write, but we're born composers.

7

Medium, Media, Mediation

My title may be too cute, but I mean by it to suggest certain questions which we need to keep in mind: "Medium, Media, Mediation." We need always to consider the relationship of the medium and the message. Marshall McLuhan's reduction of one to the other was a brilliant figure of speech about certain uses of language, but it is generally taken rather literally; that is often the fate of metaphors. When we speak of The Media, we don't generally mean the plural of *medium* —the term as it's used, say, of an artist's watercolor or clay— but, rather, those who use one or another medium. Of course, we know the difference between the TV tube and the quiz-show master or the opera star whose electronically conveyed image we watch. My point is that a single term covers both the means and the user, despite the fact that the way we receive information and the attitudes and loyalties and indebtedness which determine what we receive are not the same sort of thing. The third term in my title, *mediation*, belongs neither to the way we get the message nor to the messenger but to the conditions under which a message comes into being: mediation has to do with the meanings that make meaning possible.

Address to the Massachusetts Council of Teachers of English, Amherst, Massachusetts, September 29, 1984.

Now any of those circularities—meanings to make meaning, form to find form, interpreting our interpretations, knowing our knowledge—these circularities scare positivists to death. They are fearful of getting caught up in what they consider to be a vicious circle and plead instead for us to get back to the facts, to the data, to the real world, to what's really happening, to the way it really is—real, real, real. Positivists do not like the idea that whatever we know comes to us by means of form; they don't like the idea of mediation, which they consider a barrier between us and reality. St. Paul is helpful on this score: we do not see face to face, as long as we are in the world of time and space; IMmediate knowledge is not given to us fallen creatures. (I find religious metaphors very helpful because the relationship of language and thought is analogous to that between the body and the soul, but this affinity gets me into trouble occasionally. Once in West Virginia I was going on in this vein and a woman came up to me afterwards and thanked me, saying how much I reminded her of the Reverend Falwell.)

All our experience is mediated, and whether you want to think of it as The Fall of Man or the species-specific character of *Homo sapiens*, the fact of the matter is that there are no data and there are no facts until and unless we *formulate* them. We then must interpret them—and then interpret our interpretations. The trout can interpret, but only Man, *Homo sapiens*, can interpret his interpretations, can know his knowledge. Indeed, the correct name for our species is *Homo sapiens sapiens: the creature who knows that he knows.*

I want, first of all, to warn that the terminology we pick up from educationists, cognitive scientists, and computer salesmen can mislead us, because we do not always recognize the ambiguities. My first anecdote concerns a report that the Boston Public Schools have decided to institute an IBM program called "Writing to Read." (They've bought 500 PCJrs, 200 full-size PCs, and 10 portables. The price wasn't given but it certainly is over a half million dollars.) I thought the program name was quite good. It recalled the wisecrack (full of wisdom) of James Slevin, who has said that whereas it used to be held that you could write only as well as you could read, it may soon be true that you can read only as well as you can write. I thought, "Wow! This looks as if someone is developing a pedagogy which can address this new state of affairs." I read on and discovered that the youngsters match sounds and letters (nothing new there) and that they then turn to—workbooks. Nevertheless, the ETS research associate who carried out a two-year study was enthusiastic: "Not only do children learn to read, but they also clearly surpass their fellow students in written expression." Now *written expression* is a highly problematic phrase: it could mean anything and everything from the judgment that a student has followed the asinine prescription "Show, don't tell" to judging that the appropriate number of cohesive ties has been deployed. I wrote the ETS research associate that I would appreciate knowing what her working concept of *written expression* was, but I never had an answer. A phrase like *written expression* has many meanings and there is no way of judging the validity of the study conducted unless we are given some notion of what was being studied. The thing about language is that you have to study it by means of language; furthermore, the careless use of language about language is far more hazardous when that language is cybernetic jargon. I will illustrate with two such terms, *code* and *information*.

Linguists often say that the speaker or writer *encodes* his message; the message is then sent and is *decoded* by the receiver or audience or reader. But that is a muddle, because what is sent is not message but signal; the signal is sent and that is the way the message is conveyed—by airwaves disturbed in a pattern, by electrical pulses, by laser wiggles, by semaphore or smoke rings. The message requires a signal, but it is not itself the signal. The signal is decoded so that the message can come to life again. The process of interpretation involves us in comparing what was sent—hypothesizing what that might be—and checking it against what we think we have got. It is a very iffy process; it requires that we keep things tentative, that we tolerate ambiguities, that we not jump to conclusions. Talk about *coding* and *decoding* can obscure the nature of interpretation because, as I. A. Richards puts it, the Morse Code is not the same sort of thing as a code of behavior.

Information presents a far worse hazard: when we speak of *information processing*, we may think that that is like getting *information* for a term paper. But the fact is that *information* in information theory—cybernetics, the theory that underlies the science of computers, communication theory—*information* there has nothing whatsoever to do with *information* as we use it in normal circumstances: "I need some more information before I can give you an answer about that."

The philosopher Max Black puts it this way: it makes absolutely no difference in terms of information theory whether your message is *Max Black is white* or *Max White is black*. With modern technology, even "Information, please" may soon be handled by coded signal. When we talk about *information processing* it's extremely important that we not confuse this with what human beings do. There's something called—God help us—the Human Information Processing Center. Juxtaposing *information processing* and *human information processing* makes it sound as if all those human activities like interpretation and understanding and comprehending can somehow be reduced and simplified and organized and controlled in such a way that they are easier to teach and easier to learn: Don't you believe it! Human information processing is a matter of making meanings and construing meanings, and we can do that only by means of other meanings.

The philosophy of language we need to guide our teaching must help us differentiate information as a code of binary oppositions and as what we want to represent and interpret. We need a triadic semiotics—a way of accounting for meaning as a three-valued relationship. The curious triangle[1] is a talisman. The next time you read something like this, it could protect you:

> "Computers can teach through demonstrating how the human mind processes information," says Assistant Professor of Psychology Thomas Lacki. His course, "Computer Models of Psychological Processes," introduces the computer as a metaphor for psychological processes such as visual perception, problem solving, memory, and language. "In some ways, computers are like the human mind," explains Lacki. "They receive, code, transfer, retrieve, and store information."

Note the terms *information* and *mind*. There's a muddle here because the way that the brain processes information can be understood in terms of information theory, whereas the way in which the mind "processes information" cannot be. We can say that the brain processes by means of binary opposition because there are plus and minus electrical charges as the neurons fire; that is why it does make sense to say, as Mirsky so inelegantly does, that the brain is a computer made of meat.

But the brain is not the mind and we should not allow computer enthusiasts to foist their confusions on us. Artificial-intelligence buffs build models without a trace of mind or spirit or intention, but there's a catch: there is no way to turn on these clean machines unless they call in a *competent* operator or add (surreptitiously) a *semantic* operator. Positivists smuggle back in precisely what they have loudly proclaimed is pure mystification. I do not mean to suggest that the mind is thing-y or that it's a ghost in the machine. Mind is the phase of brain activity which we feel; hence the title of Susanne K. Langer's masterpiece, *Mind: An Essay on Human Feeling.* For the time being, I think it is useful to think of this ratio:

Mind:Brain :: Soul:Body :: Message:Signal

I've been talking so far about the hazards of the language we use about language, how we can get trapped and tricked by the terms we use. The jargon of cybernetics is hard to resist because it makes people who teach "the language arts" feel a little more respectable. A supervisor from the South Shore recently remarked to the NCTE Commission on Composition that English classes have to be scheduled to accommodate double periods for math but that principals don't see any problem there because math is solid fare and obviously has priority, whereas English is "enrichment." I think this misconception derives from the Killer Dichotomy of the so-called Cognitive and Affective Domains. That's my favorite hobby horse and I won't go on about it just now, but to represent what I have in mind, let me draw your attention to a typical headline, this one from *Time* magazine a couple of years ago: "The Fuzzies meet the Techs." And guess who the Fuzzies are? They're us, of course. And the Techs are, allegedly, scientists who are thought to be dealing with The Facts and The Real World: *they* don't have to concern themselves with Meaning or Mediation. Measuring the table is supposed to be an act which is real, but describing the table is seen as a merely relative, merely personal matter. This dichotomy of explanation and description obscures the fact that to measure anything you need a criterion or standard and that is a mediating factor. A yardstick works because we have an interpretant, constituted by the concept of measurement according to inches and feet. If you look carefully in the corner wall of Trafalgar Square, you'll find the standard foot for the British Empire, originally calculated in terms of the British soldier's stride, which perhaps originally was in imitation of the stride of the Roman legionnaire's. Inches, feet, and yards are mapped on the human body; metrical measurements are calculated in terms of distances from the North Pole to the Equator. Centimeters and kilometers are mapped, as it were, on the Earth's surface so that the Earth's surface can be mapped. All measurement is mediation; that's why it can be meaningful. The point gets lost because positivists embrace the idea that measurement is direct and IMmediate.

Now this affects us, since the common extrapolation is that science is "real" and the humanities are "fuzzy" because the values in terms of which we make meanings are not set in cement, not in Trafalgar Square or any other place. Thus we get the idea that scientists can't appreciate what we do. But that is not necessarily true. *Real* scientists understand very well that their observations are dependent on their instruments, the means which provide the means of making meaning. Dixie Goswami has observed that it's generally the scientists who understand the idea of writing as a mode of learning—or they understand it more readily than humanists who have been brainwashed into thinking of themselves as the Fuzzies or who have decided that by worshipping the Idols of the Laboratory they will be taken seriously. And it is certainly true that grants are more likely to go to proposals which promise numbers than to those which aim for new pedagogies. But real scientists, who are not just technologists, realize that their ideas are mediated, just as ours are; they realize that there is no such thing as The Data, waiting out there to be captured—nonverbal butterflies to be captured in verbal or numerical butterfly nets. Real, practicing scientists realize that the data come to them by courtesy of both their instruments and those mediating ideas which enable them to make sense of what the lens focuses. I. A. Richards called such mediating ideas "speculative instruments." They are the means by which we, scientists and humanists alike, make sense of what we study, both pointer readings and images; they make possible the representations of our experience, both models and metaphors.

Becoming alert to the hazards of computer jargon can help us set aside the spurious claims made for educational technology. We will then be able to assess more clearly and rigorously just what advantages there might be in computers for writers and teachers of writing. I will list briefly what I think computers can help us do, adding a caveat here and there.

1. Several people have convinced me that working directly on the computer keyboard helps them get the flow of words started. I think there are other ways of getting words started which don't cost as much as a word processor, but anything that can get us to syntax is praiseworthy. It is the tendency of words toward syntax which makes discourse possible; it is the discursive power of language that brings thought along with it. If word processing can help a writer toward fluency, then it is a good thing, but I hope I've persuaded you that information processing will not necessarily aid whatever we mean by human information processing.

2. Lil Brannon and Cy Knoblauch presented a paper at the MLA making the case that a word processor facilitates collaborative writing. Their marriage followed the composition of that paper and validates it emblematically.

3. An interesting case has been made for the use of electronic mail to monitor the work in progress of composition students, but it seems to me an intolerable way to begin or end a day, checking the electronic mail to see how 22 papers are coming along. I think there's a good chance that the ease of making progress reports can forestall the hard work of learning how to frame the options.

4. Angela Dorenkamp remarked recently that "the computer is going to save us from those who perceive spelling and punctuation as writing. Once students can put everything through spelling and punctuation programs, teachers will HAVE to deal with composing." Chris Parkhurst of UMass/Boston has gone further than that: she's developed a program for ESL students in which mechanics and meaning are continually brought into conjunction. Hers is the only program I've seen which involves the student in thinking about the relationship of answers to new questions; it focuses on the relationship of syntax and semantics and leads students to formulate their own questions.

5. Finally, the computer could be a fascinating research tool and heuristic, if ever anyone could understand how to do with grammar and syntax and the lexicon what Jeanne Bamberger has done with pitch, rhythm, and notation. (Her research is briefly mentioned in an interview I conducted with the composer Joyce Mekeel; it appears in the final section of *Reclaiming*

the Imagination, "Artists at Work.") Jeanne Bamberger has
experimented with using the computer for "exploring multiple
descriptions and for confronting incongruencies among them"
in the field of music. She writes:

The computer can be a powerful tool for encouraging this
kind of cognitive risk-taking by becoming an arena for
making *multiple descriptions* of some small world of phe-
nomena, each description capturing different features and
relations and thus suggesting new meanings which transform your intuitive knowledge.[2]

In another ingenious program developed in the early 1970s,
Marie Boroff of Yale University demonstrated how the computer could convert poetry to an instrument for research into
how words work.[3] She composed a program called "Random
Stanza" in which a computer "was made to generate 'poetic
imagery' arranged in stanzaic free-verse patterns." "I designed
this program," she wrote, "to obtain a maximum of vividness
and originality in a grammatically, if not rationally, coherent
language clearly affiliated with poetry rather than with prose."
A poem called "The Meditation of IBM 7094-7040" includes
such lines as these:

Let the tautology of your arm
Be reddened;
Let the way of your hat
Be dissolved.

And

In the evening of substance
Expansively, restlessly,
The beaches pray.

The delight in watching quasi-meanings emerge from coherent
syntactical structures is matched by the curiosity that develops
about what different limits would allow, different words and
different slots. I can testify that students do learn something
about syntax at the same time that they are learning how poetic
diction functions. I often distribute to my classes what I call
a Machine for Making a Toy Poem. There is a set of slots, nine
different categories of words which are to be slotted and a guide

which suggests a sequence of slotting. Once the schema is completed, you have a do-it-yourself haiku and what is learned is rather more substantial than what is learned in the usual haiku session. The empty structure reads like this:

All _____ in the _____,
I _____ _____ _____ in the _____.
_____! The _____ has _____.

　　　All green in the leaves
　　　I smell dark pools in the trees
　　　Crash! The moon has fled.

This requires no word processor, though the processing procedure is analogous to a computer program. It can help students discover the heuristic power of language itself, to study how the image-making power of language and the discursive power of language make the making of meaning possible.

The easiest way to encourage this discovery is to have students provide themselves with their own personal computers, in the form of a dialectical notebook. On one side, observations are recorded, passages are copied out, drawings are made and notes and jottings—anything by which impressions and ideas can be represented. On the other side, on the facing page, notes about notes are written, observations of observations. In this way, students are practicing recording that very dialectic which constitutes the inner dialogue we call thinking. These little human information processors are not ticking away with 0/1, pro/con, yes/no, on again/off again. They are interpreting their interpretations and seeing what meanings have enabled them to discover meanings and to make further meanings. They will be learning to take advantage of that allatonceness which characterizes the composing process. The dialectical notebook—the double-entry journal—encourages those habits of mind most needed by writers: the ability to look and look again; to question answers and to formulate new questions which will lead to new answers; to tolerate ambiguity; to take cognitive risks, if you like the concept Jeanne Bamberger deploys; to know one's knowledge, as Coleridge put it. Above all, this kind of notebook enables students to discover the power of language itself and thereby the power of their own minds. Keeping a dialectical notebook helps reclaim imagination, which is so often debased by those who think of it as a fantasy generator, without realizing that it is the forming power of mind, "the prime agent of all human perception."

Notes

1. See Prologue.
2. "The Art of Cognitive Risk-Taking," in *Papers from Invitational Conference on Innovation and Productivity in Higher Education,* (San Francisco: San Francisco Press, 1977), 63–65.
3. See Marie Borroff, "Computer as Poet," *Yale Alumni Magazine,* January 1971; and "Creativity, Poetic Language, and the Computer," *The Yale Review,* LX (1971), 481–513.

III

Is Reading Still Possible?

Yes—if we recognize that it is a hermeneutic enterprise.

*　　*　　*

We will need to defend against the newest gangster theory, which is that reading should be taught on the model of defensive driving: "Look out! What are they putting over on you? Can't you see you're being manipulated?" Those who have abandoned instruction as a necessarily oppressive concept are turning from the study of literature to a no-fault decoding of "texts" or to the mystic variant of this neopositivist strategy, viz., the encouragement of solipsistic "response" which theoretically cannot be analyzed, corrected, or revised, since all meaning is "indeterminate." If "literacy studies" can help to reclaim reading as a critical and creative act of mind and as an activity of incomparable political importance, we will be fortunate indeed. Meanwhile, it is perhaps not too late to reexamine and renew the defense of poetry as offering instruction and delight.

Anything which is learned about reading, considered in a triadic perspective, will be pertinent to learning to write. That is because both reading and writing are activities impelled by "the sense of learning," the inborn, species-specific capacity to recognize, to form, to abstract, to represent,—and to re-represent. I believe that if we set aside the conviction that the way to teach reading is to test "comprehension" and that the way to teach writing is to assign topics (complete with Study

105

Questions); if we abandon the pedagogy of exhortation (which is a variant of the pedagogy of the oppressor, the one who knows what you should know); if we can finally liberate ourselves from both positivist and mystic versions of a view of meaning as substance or essence or code, we might then be free to move toward what Paulo Freire calls a "pedagogy of knowing," a philosophy of education which sees reading and writing as ways of recognizing representations, of representing recognitions.

8

Is Reading Still Possible?

Whether or not it's significant I don't know, but it surely is remarkable that a public concern for literacy (however understood) is being expressed at the same time that we are seeing in the academy the apotheosis of the doctrine that all reading is misreading. What this coincidence perhaps suggests is a deep uncertainty about what it means to be able to read and write, both in the sense of how we define those acts and how we judge their importance. That uncertainty is at the root of controversies of the past forty years or so about how reading should be taught and I think it is discernible in current discussions of literacy.

If we are, once again, to be able to differentiate variant readings from misreading—as I. A. Richards put it—and if we are to confront the challenge of illiteracy, we will need a new orientation. In my view, that orientation should take the form not of academic exercises in definition, the kind English teachers are so fond of—"What IS English?" "What IS Literacy?" "What IS Reading?"—but of authentic problem posing. What kind of understanding of meaning, of representation, of interpretation, of process, of method—and so on—do we need in order to teach reading and writing as modes of learning and

Certain passages in this chapter appear in "Reading In/Reading Out," in *Farther Along: Transforming Dichotomies in Rhetoric and Composition*, ed. Kate Ronald and Hephzibah Roskelly (Portsmouth, NH: Boynton/Cook, 1990).

ways of knowing? What difference would one or another theory of the sign make to the way we organize the curriculum and design our courses? If we account for meaning in triadic terms, how will that change the accounts we give of meaning?

Asking such questions—posing such problems—constitutes the orientation I mean. They require that we turn away from presuppositions about language and discourse which have been accepted uncritically for so long. I. A. Richards, in calling for a "new" rhetoric in 1936, declared that rhetoric "must take charge of the criticism of its own assumptions." It's about time for that to begin to happen.

I want to claim that reading—like writing, like teaching—is a hermeneutic enterprise. When we read critically—which is to say when we read for meaning—we interpret, necessarily. A triadic semiotics can guide us in thinking of reading as a process of making meaning and in recognizing that process as entailing interpretation. Interpretation is a dialectical activity because we are continually discovering the interinanimation of words and thereby the interdependence of what is said and what is meant. When we read, we don't decode and then figure out what is being said any more than we figure out what we want to say when we write and then encode it.

Reading and writing are at once personal and social activities: we can no more separate the individual and the general aspects of meaning making than we can the *how* and the *what*. That is not to say that these dialectical pairs cannot be *differentiated*: the point is that they are not *separate*, dichotomous, or antithetical. Triadicity, as an idea to think *with*, can help remind us that reading for meaning requires that we bring meanings to the text in order to take away further, other meanings. Triadicity offers the best defense against the Killer Dichotomy of *reading in/reading out*. The notion that first students must figure out "what the author is trying to say" and then they can interpret by reading in their own experience is profoundly mistaken.

When we read, we construct and construe simultaneously. We construe the graphic code and the syntactical structures by means of the meanings we expect to be represented. Or, rather, that is what happens when we are really reading, making meaning. It might well be a common experience of grade-school teachers, but I have myself only once heard someone "read" without the mediation of meanings. I don't mean slow reading, sounding the words subvocally, moving your lips; I mean construing letter by letter, without the guidance of expectation, without imagination, without interpretation. I witnessed this in Wales where my family spent a year when I was a child. Sunday School was not playing quiet games and making models of the Holy Land, as I was used to doing; it was reading aloud from the Scriptures. There in that bone-chilling church—what they call the "new" chapel dates from the twelfth century—I heard children read word by word; each word, letter by letter. All these years that has remained with me as an image of meaningless activity—mindless and spirit-killing. The very antithesis is provided by Paulo Freire's account of how he learned to read the world, attending to stages of the ripening of mangoes (see pp. 119–20). It wasn't because there were no mangoes in their backyards that the Welsh children weren't really reading from the Book of Esther or the Gospel according to Saint Luke. It was because they had been taught to read by the letter and not by the word—"word" understood as meaning "an element of meaning." The fact that the word *word* is a radical metaphor for meaning as well as for a single grammatical element is itself an emblem of what Freire means when he draws the analogy between reading the world and reading the word. *Reading* works as a metaphor for interpretation because what we do with language is fundamentally the same as what we do in perception, in making sense of the world. Saying and seeing are both ways of forming, ways of knowing, ways of making meaning.

If we want our students to see how construing a text entails constructing meaning, we will need to focus on the relationship of what is written and what is meant. All reading, that is to say, is like translating from one language to another. Translation, as Richards realized, provides an excellent model for the reading process since it is never a matter of substituting one word for another; it always requires what he came to call "comparison fields"—overlapping contexts, grounds for analogies and metaphors, linguistic or experiential commonalties (*Reclaiming* 176). The extraordinary thing about Richards' ideas of how translation works is that he developed them pedagogically. As readers explore the range of meaning of the words of the text and the kinds of divisions and differentiation definition requires, they are letting the process of construing guide and direct the process of constructing—and vice versa: the meanings we are making become the means of reviewing the meanings we have made.

The best description of this process which Richards offers comes, interestingly enough, in the following comment on composition:

> Composition is the supplying at the right time and place of whatever the developing meaning then and there requires. It is the cooperation with the rest in preparing for what is to come and completing what has preceded. It is more than this, though; it is the exploration of what is to come and of how it should be prepared for, and it is the further examination of what has preceded and of how it may be amended and completed (*So Much Nearer* 119–20).

I believe that there will be a revolution in the teaching of English when the realization is won—it will not simply dawn—that reading can best be taught as we teach writing— "as" meaning both "at the same time" and "in the same enlightened ways."

If the first priority for writers is, as I believe, to learn to tolerate chaos, then analogously the reader must learn to tolerate ambiguity, to allow for competing meanings to develop. The chief reason for reading substantial, complex prose—and reading it slowly—is that it provides opportunities for developing certain habits of questioning, of looking and looking again, and for practicing certain procedures for auditing meanings which are in competition. These habits are not "subskills" but attitudes which are nurtured by "the sense of learning." The general run of textbooks do not help on this score: organization is by typography; there is little subordination and lots of paratactic assertion. There is seldom a chance for the rhythm of thought to develop; *that* is dependent on dialectic, on the continuing audit of meaning, the rhythm of particularization and generalization. Textbooks do not trust the dialectic and rely, instead, on roadsigns: *The three main functions of the enzyme are. . . . Let us turn now to the second example. . . .*

Quasi-translation exercises offer the best way to remedy the deficiency of not having had the experience of translating from or into a foreign language. (Ann Raimes has seen the pedagogical possibilities in the fact that ESL students are necessarily "translators.") Whatever instruction in grammar most students have had is, generally speaking, detached from any discursive purpose. Few indeed have had practice in rewriting with attention focused on how changes in sentence structure change the way a text can be read. A debased New Criticism has made paraphrase taboo. Diagramming, which can be valuable in helping students attend to the interdependence of words in a sentence, has been scorned—on the left, because it has seemed merely mechanical, and on the right, because it is not mechanical enough. The best exercise in what has been called "vertical translation" is Phyllis Brooks's "persona paraphrase," in which students try to sound like an author by imitating his or her syntactical structures, with a different subject matter.[1] This exercise makes construing as compelling as any other aspect of interpretation by challenging students to attend to purposes. They read as prospective writers and are thus interested in the author's problems and solutions.

Reading and writing both depend on having a framework of expectations to guide procedure. To imagine what might be coming next is a universal human capacity; we do not need to teach our students how to anticipate, but we should provide opportunities for them to discover *that* they do so in making sense of the world. Learning to listen is practice in deliberate anticipation. The enterprise of reclaiming the imagination should include dictation and having students attend to a text while it is read aloud. Two "channels" are better than one because each strengthens the other. The poor quality of our students' notetaking is only the converse of poor reading. They often do not know how to record and listen simultaneously because they have not learned to imagine what's coming. Without a practiced capacity for anticipation, for envisagement, the alternative is a frantic attempt to capture complete sentences, the recording of incomplete or unintelligible lists, or simply noting scattered dates and phrases, without context or direction.

Anything learned about notetaking will be helpful in learning to read critically, in maintaining the dialectic of construing and constructing. Multiple definition, interpretive paraphrase, persona paraphrase, parody, glossing, and all other such techniques can aid students in distinguishing variant readings from misreading. That is not, of course, a matter of intuition but of accounting for what has been written in as many contexts as are found useful. Learning how texts and contexts answer one another; how feedback and feedforward work together; how words work interdependently with other words—such practical criticism will gradually help students abandon the idea that opinion about what is being read needn't be argued, that gut reactions are the only authentic form of appreciation. (Indeed, practical criticism could also rescue teachers who are *enthralled*—the root meaning is *caught up in, imprisoned*—by poststructuralist theory that denies the possibility of reference, representation, interpretation, and, finally, of literary meaning itself.) As they learn to support their interpretations, students will also be learning that although all knowledge is mediated, it does not follow that any opinion or interpretation is as good as another. "Relativism" has gotten a bad name because of a failure to establish the principle that fallibilism—Peirce's term for the acknowledgment that since we do not see face to face, we can never know for sure—does not mean "anything goes."

At the conference on style which occasioned Jakobson's famous "closing statement" in which he set forth his definition of poetry in terms of syntagmatic and paradigmatic axes, I. A. Richards read two papers, "Poetic Process and Literary Analysis" and "Variant Readings and Misreading." He has some very amusing things to say about the "reckless disregard of all the means by which language defends itself" and some important things to say about how the risk of error might be controlled and how misreading is connected to the way reading is taught. His observations about the limitations which the linguistic system imposes on any one component are based, typically, on the metaphor of discourse as a state which must be organized, controlled, and protected. I quote from the closing paragraphs:

> A linguistics that is properly aware of the processes through which language grows in the individual and of the effects that his attitudes to language can have upon its health in him must be concerned with pedagogy and with what sorts of assumptions are spread in the school. . . . For the purposes outlined above and on the appropriate occasions, may *misreading* mean the taking of a sentence in such a way that the equivalence relations of one or more of its parts to the rest of the language lapse and thereby, if such taking were to continue, harm would be done to language—due regard, however, being given in applying this criterion to the necessity for change in language activity with change in the situation to be met, and, in general, to the health of the language (*So Much Nearer* 198).

I. A. Richards is a thoughtful, provocative, cheerful, inventive, encouraging guide to all who engage in practical criticism, but if we want to consider the consequences of his conviction that literacy is essential to the survival of the planet, we will need to supplement our reading of Richards with the study of those whose pedagogy takes into account the social contexts of meaning. The two most important are, I believe, Paulo Freire and Louise Rosenblatt; in the chapters which follow, I will consider certain aspects of their pedagogies.

Richards, Freire, and Rosenblatt are all pragmatists, which means that they ask not "Does it work?" or "Can we afford it?" but "What difference would it make to our practice if we proceeded from these principles?" And it is equally true that they are all three alert to what Rosenblatt calls "the common life of humanity"; to what Richards, citing Coleridge, calls "the all-in-each of human nature"; to what Freire recognizes in Man's character as a creature not only of Nature but of History. We read Richards, Rosenblatt, and Freire not because they are "reading specialists," but because their passionately held convictions can guide us in reclaiming the imagination, understood as the power of the active mind.

Note

1. From "Mimesis: Grammar and the Echoing Voice," *College English* 35 (November 1973), 161–68.

9

"Reading the World . . . Reading the Word"

Paulo Freire's Pedagogy of Knowing

Paulo Freire warns against sloganeering, in which words substitute for critical thinking; but mottoes and maxims by which we may formulate critical attitudes are something else. Freire is himself a superb aphorist, like I. A. Richards, whom he curiously resembles—curiously, because though they come from markedly different backgrounds and do not in the least sound like each other, they nevertheless see eye to eye about the nature of language and learning; about the urgency of comprehending the significance of illiteracy the world around; about the character of the pedagogy which will be required if the political challenge posed by illiteracy is to be met. When Freire juxtaposes *reading the world* and *reading the word*, he identifies, it seems to me, the only foundation upon which literacy can be firmly established, and that is interpretation, seen as the act of making meaning. *Reading the world* and *reading the word* brought thus into analogous conjunction become models for one another and they can do so because they belong to that family of radical metaphors, the chief of which is seeing as a way of knowing and knowing as both insight and the power of envisagement. Knowledge, Coleridge said, is "vision nascent."

The springs of Freire's wisdom are in nineteenth-century

From *Only Connect*, ed. Thomas Newkirk (Portsmouth, NH: Boynton/Cook, 1986).

political thought and the New Testament; that's why his ideas can sound familiar to us, though his guides might not be our own. Occasionally he deploys the language of Marxism, but not in a doctrinaire fashion, for he has his own versions of what is entailed in *praxis, dialectic, oppression, revolution,* and *struggle* so that the words themselves serve new purposes, thereby taking on new meanings. The same holds for his deployment of the lexicon of Christianity. Richard Horsley, professor of religion at UMass/Boston, has remarked that after hearing Freire at the Harvard Divinity School in the early 1970s, he began reading the New Testament in a completely new way. Of course, to read Scripture dialectically is nothing new; typology is nothing if not dialectical. Freire is one of the mentors of liberation theology the world over because his pedagogy of knowing provides a method by which such powers of interpretation are made accessible to all who can learn. He is a profoundly traditional man, but no one should think that reading Freire is an exercise in surveying received ideas. He transforms whatever he uses; every idea gains in significance as he develops contexts and draws out implications. Freire is not only a superb theoretician: he is one of the great teachers of the century. We can learn from him because his conception of education as a pedagogy of knowing helps us teach reading and writing as interpretive acts and thus helps us comprehend our comprehensions of literacy more comprehensively.

Forming the concept of literacy, which is to say, thinking about what we mean when we define the relationship of reading and writing to each other and to language, considered biologically and philosophically as a species-specific power, is not the same thing as formulating an unambiguous definition. "What IS literacy?" would not be an advantageous point of departure, and yet we must ask over and over again what we mean when we consider the relationship of reading and writing to each other and of each to the private and public uses of language, to the functions of language so often forgotten by rhetoricians and linguists, viz., expression and representation. I want to begin by claiming that when literacy is reduced to meaning manipulation of the graphic code, the consequences can be hazardous. Consider these cases.

The dean of a college which has developed a competency-based program was recently very reluctant to expand support for a skills center. "Why should our students have to write at all?" he asked. "They are very good talkers. Let them use tape

recorders." An ignorant remark—one might almost say an illiterate remark—but it expresses a view which is not at all
uncommon and is certainly not limited to the leftover radicals
of American education. In Kenya, for instance, the universities
have been closed. Daniel arap Moi, the virtually illiterate successor of Jomo Kenyatta, has decided that higher education is
not a priority for Kenya; indeed, education at all levels has been
neglected—but that is too mild a term: education has been
virtually forgotten. In the schools there is no chalk, no paper
or pens. (The fifty-shilling note nevertheless depicts a multi-
racial group of youngsters sitting on the ground reading to one
another.) Instruction is generally by drill, with blows on the
knuckles for errors—a parody of the worst educational practice
of former colonial masters. In some instances, teachers stress
the oral tradition. They urge their students, when they return
to their shambas on the weekends, to have their grannies tell
them stories. But the grannies don't know any stories; the oral
tradition is no more alive in Nairobi and its environs than it
is in those institutes on orality where English teachers huddle
by the ski-lodge fire, trying to tell stories to one another. Ken-
yans are caught between two cultures, one powerless to be born
as long as those in power turn all inadequacies and insuffi-
ciencies to their ideological purpose. I believe the same sort of
judgment could be made of the students victimized by the
aforementioned dean.

Ideologues for whom it is important to discount the value
of literacy could find support for their views in the research of
Michael Cole and Sylvia Scribner. In an attempt to isolate literacy from schooling and to identify and differentiate the effects of each, they studied a tribe in Western Africa which has
had a syllabic script for a hundred and fifty years, a form of
writing employed only by certain males and limited to com-
mercial purposes, chiefly accounting, as in the case of Sumerian
clay tablets, and to the composition of letters which are as
conventionalized as a Berlitz phrase book. It is entirely ex-
pectable, then, that Cole and Scribner should conclude as follows:

> We did not find literacy in the Vai script associated with
> generalized competence that might be characterized as
> abstraction or verbal reasoning or metalinguistic skills.
> The situation with regard to reading and writing is not

dissimilar from that of other skilled practices such as weaving and pottery-making.[1]

I am amused at the echo here of Cardinal Newman's judgment that since music has no intellectual or moral value it should be relegated to the class of harmless but worthless activities, along with the stuffing of birds.

These conceptions of literacy are certainly impoverished: one identifies writing with the graphic means of representing sound, which is then easily dismissed as less efficient than a tape recorder and less authentic than speech; the other assumes that literacy can be represented by communicative functions which are absolutely minimal. Reading and writing are thus demeaned when the underlying view of language is restrictive. Those who consider reading and writing as "technologies" generally consider language itself as, simply, a communication medium and knowledge, a matter of information processing, or in its soft form, *"human* information processing."

These reductive views of literacy are, however, scarcely more harmful than the stretching that is done in the case of "cultural literacy." The test of any idea should be what it can do for us, and the notion of "cultural literacy," as far as I can see, has led to no new thinking about the relationship of reading and writing; it fosters no new ideas about how to read a book, much less about how to read a page: "cultural literacy" has nothing whatsoever to do with pedagogy. It is helping to persuade people that something can be done about illiteracy in America if only we can get high school students to read Fifty Good Books in their summer vacations so that they'll be ready for One Hundred Great Books in college.

Both reducing and stretching what we mean by *literacy* yields pseudo-concepts, in Vygotsky's sense. The only way we can protect ourselves from the ill effects of such misrepresentations is to be good pragmatists: how we use an idea, how it invites us to put it into practice, will tell us best what the significance of the idea is. English teachers will come into their own when they realize that it is pedagogy, and not psycholinguistics and cognitive psychology, which provides the authentic means of discovering, as Richards puts it, "what we are trying to do and thereby how to do it" (*Design for Escape* 111).

For Paulo Freire, as for I. A. Richards, Maria Montessori,

William James, and other great teachers, theory and practice
are mutually supportive, generating one another, each offering
the means of critical revision of the other. Freire's *method* thus
brings theory and practice together and keeps them in conjunction. I want to turn now to considering how his
pedagogy—his method—is informed by a philosophically sound
view of language and is inspirited by that unsentimental respect
for human beings which only a sound philosophy of mind can
assure.

Freire's pedagogy is the antithesis of that spoonfeeding of
letters and attitudes which Sartre scornfully called "alimentary
education." ("Here! Swallow this! It'll be good for you!") The
digestive theory of education is inescapably authoritarian: the
teacher knows what's good for you. It requires passive subjects
who are in no sense creators of knowledge. A pedagogy of knowing converts learners to agents who are actively aware of what
they are doing. Peasants and teacher are engaged in dialogic
action, an active exchange from which meanings emerge and
are seen to emerge. It is central to Freire's pedagogy that learners are empowered by the *knowledge that* they are learners.[2]
This conscientization or "critical consciousness,"—this
awareness of oneself as a knower, as meaning maker—is brought
into being in the course of dialogue, which is, Freire has written, "the encounter between men to name the world." The
learners are engaged continually in thinking about thinking,
in those reflective acts of interpreting interpretations which
language makes possible. We are so used to thinking of language
as a "communication medium" that sometimes it can be a
surprise to discover, or to be reminded, that language is the
means of making those meanings which we communicate.
Freire's pedagogy is founded on a philosophical understanding
of this generative power of language. When we speak, the discursive power of language—its tendency toward syntax—brings
thought along with it. We don't think our thoughts and then
put them into words: we say and mean at the same time;
utterance and meaning making are simultaneous and correlative.

The principles of conscientization and dialogic action are
given substance and authenticity by the philosophy of language
which undergirds them. The pedagogy of knowing is empowered by the principle that naming the world entails identifying
and classifying and that by those acts of mind learners are
engaged in making meanings. The act of naming, of speaking

the word, entails the naming of the world: "Human beings," Freire said at U Mass/Boston, "did not start by calling A! F! N! They first freed the hand and grasped the world." (Freire would know what Emerson meant in speaking of "the hand of the mind.") This understanding of the etiology of naming is biologically and philosophically grounded in a conception of man as the language animal, the *animal symbolicum*. And, indeed, to turn from a study of Freire's pedagogy of knowing to a study of Cassirer's *Essay on Man*, setting forth his philosophy of symbolic form, or to Susanne K. Langer's *Mind: An Essay on Human Feeling* is like hearing variations on a theme.

In a recent talk to a conference on reading in Brazil, Freire recounted how in writing his text—the text of his remarks— he had "recreated and lived," as he says, "the experience I lived at a time when I did not yet read words." Here is the passage in which Freire tells of reading that early world:

> I see myself then in the average Recife house where I was born, encircled by trees. Some of the trees were like persons to me, such was the intimacy between us. In their shadow I played, and in the branches accessible to my height I experienced the small risks which prepared me for greater risks and adventures. The old house, its bedrooms, hall, attic, terrace—the setting for my mother's ferns—the back yard where the terrace was located, all this was my first world. In this world I crawled, gurgled, first stood up, took my first steps, said my first words. Truly, that special world presented itself to me as the arena of my perceptual activity, and therefore as the world of my first reading. The *texts*, the *words*, the *letters* of that context were incarnated in a series of things, objects, signs. In perceiving these, I experienced myself, and the more I experienced myself, the more my perceptual capacity increased. I learned to understand things, objects, signs through using them in relationship to my older brothers and sisters and my parents.
>
> The *texts*, *words*, *letters* of that context were incarnated in the song of the birds—tanager, flycatcher, thrush; in the dance of boughs blown by the strong winds announcing storms; thunder and lightning; rain waters playing with geography: creating lakes, islands, rivers, streams. The *texts*, *words*, *letters* of the context were incarnated as well in the whistle of the wind, the clouds of the sky,

the sky's color, its movement; in the color of foliage, the shape of leaves, the fragrance of flowers—roses, jasmine; in tree trunks; in fruit rinds: the varying color tones of the same fruit at different times—the green of a mango when the fruit is first forming, the green of a mango fully formed, the greenish yellow of the same mango ripening, the black spots of an overripe mango—the relationship among these colors, the developing fruit, its resistance to our manipulation, and its taste. It was possibly at this time, by doing it myself and seeing others do it, that I learned the meaning of the word *squashing.*

Animals were equally part of that context—the way the family cats rubbed themselves coyly against our legs, their mewing of entreaty or anger; the ill-humor of Joli, my father's old black dog, when one of the cats carelessly approached too near to where he was eating what was his. In such instances, Joli's mood was completely different from when he rather sportively chased, caught, and killed one of the many opossums responsible for the disappearance of my grandmother's fat chickens.

Part of the context of my immediate world was also the language universe of my elders, expressing their beliefs, tastes, fears, values, and which linked my world to wider contexts whose existence I could not even suspect (*The Politics of Education* 30–31).

Freire's pedagogy of knowing is based on the principle that all human beings read the world; we all make sense of our experience, construing and constructing and representing it by means of language. His pedagogy takes advantage of the fact that imagination is "the prime agent of all human perception," that the forming power of mind is God-given and species-specific.

Freire's real work as a teacher began when he faced the fact that beginning with vowel sounds—*ba, be, bi, bo, bu*—was not the way to proceed with the people he was trying to reach, the peasants of Brazil. Many people note the fact, but few ever face it—I mean the fact that the elements into which a process can be analyzed do not themselves constitute the process nor do they, lined up, offer a model for the way in which a process can best be learned. Tolstoy recognized the fact, faced it, and set it down this way: "To the teacher the simplest and most general appears easiest—pigs, pots, a table

—whereas for the pupil, only the complex and living appears easy." Freire's genius has been to begin with pigs and pots in such a way that they become significant, the bearers of import, representative and emblematic. Tolstoy's method—discovered by chance—was to give his pupils a proverb for which they then imagined the agents and action, the setting and events, thus creating the incarnation of its meaning.[3] Freire, too, begins with narrative which is not merely psychological, merely personal. His method is to "problematize the existential situation," to lead the would-be learners to transform the scenes and events, the dull routines of their lives, so that unexamined answers become provocative questions. As the peasants who have joined the culture circles look and look again at the actuality of their lives, recognizing the meanings represented by a picture of a squalid kitchen or a bowl of dirty water, they come to questions—not to problem solving but to problem posing.

One measure of the success of this method of literacy training is that Freire was exiled: the step from a personal narrative, recounting orally a childhood experience of carrying water from a stream a mile distant, to descriptions of dirty water from the local pump led to further questions about the taxes paid for the use of that pump. At the heart of Freire's pedagogy of knowing is the idea that naming the world becomes a model for changing the world. (Indeed, Freire seems to be playing with the terms of Marx's famous slogan, that the aim should no longer be to explain but to change.) Education does not substitute for political action, but it is indispensable to it because of the role it plays in the development of critical consciousness. That, in turn, is dependent on the transforming power of language.

In naming the world, the peasants of the culture circles are asked to survey their farms and villages and to collect the names of tools, places, and activities which are of central importance in their lives. The collections differ from village to village, but in every list of generative words, Freire includes the word for *vote* and the word for *atom bomb*. (Does this help explain why the CIA cooperated when the police burned his primers and broke his slide projectors?) These "generative words" are then organized in "discovery cards," a kind of vowel grid, a do-it-yourself lexicon generator. Some of the words it produces are nonsense; others are recognizable when sounded. The crucial point is that sound and letter shape are matched with each other and with meaning or the possibility of meaning. Instead of reducing literacy to a matter of manipulating the graphic code or beginning with the process of learning the relation of letter to sound—*ba, be, bi, bo, bu*—Freire's pedagogy of knowing ensures that this decoding is always carried out simultaneously with the making of meaning: *reading the word* and *reading the world*. He differentiates *decoding*—matching sound and letter shape—from *decodification*, which is interpretation, *in order to ensure that they not be pedagogically separated*. This careful distinction between the signal which is decoded and the message which is decodified is precisely the opposite of what happens when we conflate *information* in the purely technical sense—absence of noise in the channel—with *information* in the sense of what can be communicated. Correlation is not the same thing as muddling. As a good dialectician, Freire divides in order to unite, an act which can remind us that the inventor of the pedagogy of knowing was a literacy expert living in ancient Greece.

Attempting to translate Freire's pedagogy, to adapt it to our classroom, is difficult because, for one thing, we have so much to unteach and because, for another, our students are often cut off from those experiences of the natural world which provide the best models of learning—or so I believe. Deeply rooted and purposeful sensory knowing has not generally been a dimension of their educational development. Our students find generalization difficult—and generalization is not the same thing as abstraction—because nobody ever taught them how to go about it, and in the modern world such teaching is absolutely necessary. Our students are uninstructed in looking and looking again at what they read and write; in noting likes and differents; in attending to what varies with what. They can *decode* their world, recognizing different brands of sneakers at forty paces, specifying the drawbacks of five varieties of car radios, and they can *decodify*: they know what these differences mean. But how many teachers have learned how to teach reading and writing on this model, to encourage them in reading the word as they read the world? How many of us have learned how to make writing serve this enterprise?

Our first task, it seems to me, is to offer our students assisted invitations to discover the naming and articulating powers of language, to see how language provides the means of making meaning. Generally speaking, our students have not had such experiences and the difficulty of collecting generative words suggests as much. That is a matter illuminated by Sylvia Ashton-Warner's account in *Spearpoint* of her American experience, of how it was impossible to proceed in Colorado as she had in New Zealand. Her work with Maori children features what she calls the "Key Vocabulary," "the captions of the dynamic life itself," her own fascinating version of generative words. In *Spearpoint*, she describes the frustration she felt when she was unable, in her Rocky Mountain infant room, to identify any key words at all. She was deeply shocked when the children stood on the guitar or refused to volunteer as chalk monitors, but when she could find no words, beyond *Mama* and the names of their pets, which generated or represented complex and living meanings, she was terrified.

But our classrooms are not infant rooms and collecting a list of generative words might not be quite the point. We do not need to teach decoding, as the elementary teacher must, but that does not mean that we needn't teach our students to look and look again—not at bunny rabbits perhaps, but at natural forms and designs, at texts and the topography of their own lives. I believe that we must begin with our students as makers of meaning, trusting to the mediation provided by perception and dialogue: as they learn to problematize the existential situation, our students will be discovering the generative powers of language. It isn't easy; indeed, I think it's probably harder to engage the attention of American undergraduates and to encourage their critical thinking than it is to bring peasants along from the point of believing that hailstones are the souls of aggrieved ancestors. But I think we must remember Freire's problematic bowl of dirty water and his significant pigs and pots. If we ask our students to name their world and we get *digital clocks* and *designer jeans*, that is one place to begin; that is a point of departure for conscientization and dialogic action. It's a lot harder than running those rap sessions which used to pass for the pedagogy of the oppressed. I can remember the shock I had in discovering that at U Mass in the early 1970s, young radical teachers—and some not so young—whose only pedagogy was to sit on the floor with their students, were claiming to be putting Freire into practice by asking their students "Did you know you're oppressed?" And I've heard accounts of how dismayed Freire was to find Harvard and Radcliffe students making banners with slogans meant to awaken the oppressed of Harvard Square.

If we begin with our students as meaning makers, what

happens is that objects of their field of vision become, slowly, emblems of their lives; trivial personal narratives of, for instance, the hassles experienced in getting to school by subway become "representative anecdotes," as Kenneth Burke puts it. And as this happens, our students are becoming critically conscious: they are learning to ask themselves not "What can I say to fulfill the requirements of this assignment—or to give the teacher what he wants?" but "What do I think about all this?" And they are learning to *return* to what they think about all that, to think about their thinking and to interpret their interpretations. These new-found powers of critical consciousness can then be exercised in the interest of initiating and sustaining the dialectic of *what is said* and *what is meant* as we read what others and what we ourselves have written. If we are to keep interpretation central, our best hope is to encourage our students to read the word as they read the world. *If we can make writing represent the processes of perception and dialogue, we will find ways of teaching composition as the kind of nonlinear process it is.* I believe that writing becomes an authentic mode of learning and way of knowing when it serves to enable students to record dialogic action and to represent the inner dialogue which is thought. If students learn to keep what I have elsewhere described as a dialectical notebook, the facing pages in dialogue with each other so that they learn to take notes on their notes, they will be learning to return to the meanings they have made, to reflect on them, discovering thereby how meanings provide the means of making further meaning. Writing dialectically encourages, as it *requires*, conscientization, the critical consciousness of oneself as meaning maker.

As we liberate ourselves from a pedagogy of exhortation, we will be free to discover our own special powers as composition teachers. Josephine Miles cheers us by remarking those powers. In one of her crisp and instructive essays entitled "The Freshman at Composition," in *Working Out Ideas: Predication and Other Uses of Language,* she first speculates about the reasons for the failure of her students to take "a responsible point of view," reminding us that

> Sentence-making is predication, and to predicate is to assert an idea, selecting and treating facts from a point of view. Paragraph-making is the development of such ideas

and the relationship between them. Composition involves an individual responsibility of thought.

She then notes that students seem not to realize that chronology—their only mode of organization—is an order or to understand "to what purpose they [are] putting it. And of the other logical orders, like implication, alternation, exemplification, they seem unaware." She then concludes as follows:

> It may be that we are so unaware ourselves of how to choose, how to co-ordinate and subordinate, how to generalize and exemplify, above all how to compose, that we cannot teach a younger generation. We may be, as the scientists have suggested to us, the victims of sheer uninterpreted data, as meaningless as can be. If we have no attitudes for our facts, we shall have no predicates for our subjects, no themes for our essays, no points for our remarks, no responsibilities for our actions.
>
> But I think the teachers of composition are the very ones who need not be so lost. They know that the subject is what the predicate makes it. They know that the human mind can take a consistent responsibility for what it has to say. They know that the selection and arrangement of materials to a purpose, a purpose weighed and evaluated, is as serious a task as can be conceived of.

Josephine Miles here summons us—we composition teachers need not be so lost—to a new prospect, a new sense of our powers and purposes, which should surely include forming the concept of literacy. She is herself one of our most trustworthy guides in the enterprise of learning to teach writing as a means of making meaning, as a way of coming to know, of working out ideas. But to let writing thus serve a pedagogy of knowing requires that we liberate ourselves from the positivist support system which is the chief cause of all our woe: I mean the assignment of packaged topics and the dependence on prefabricated study questions and courses of study; I mean the use of linear models which do not and cannot represent the dialectical character of composing; I mean a trivialized conception of heuristics as problem solving which ignores both the role of problem posing and the heuristic power of language; I mean the dependence on a defunct rhetoric of categories arranged in dichotomous pairs like narrative-exposition and description-definition; I mean a conception of empirical research in which what can be measured becomes by default what it is important to teach. But it is exhilarating to remember that the pedagogy of knowing not only requires liberation from positivism and scientism; it brings it about.

Paulo Freire's ideas are accessible and adaptable: if we can reconstitute our professional meetings as culture circles and our journals as authentic forums, we can begin to hear from one another about all attempts to develop a pedagogy of knowing. We will surely be engaged in forming the concept of literacy and thereby we will eventually change the state of affairs.

Let me close with one of Freire's characteristically optimistic contemplations from his talk at U Mass/Boston:

> For me, philosophically, existentially, the fundamental task of human beings should be reading the world, writing the world; reading the words, writing the words. If we did that consciously, with a critical consciousness, of course we would be active, willing, choosing subjects of history. Then we could speak freely about our presence in the world.

Notes

1. Michael Cole and Sylvia Scribner, "Literacy Without Schooling: Testing for Intellectual Effects," *Harvard Educational Review*, 48 (1978), 448–61.
2. The complex relationship of knowing *how* and knowing *that* is analogous, of course, to the relationship of practice and theory. Freire's argument is based on a thorough understanding of man as a historical being. It is set forth most substantially in Chapter Three of *Pedagogy of the Oppressed* (New York: Herder and Herder, 1970).
3. I have discussed some of the implications for composition pedagogy in "Tolstoy, Vygotsky, and the Making of Meaning," reprinted in *The Making of Meaning*.

10

Democratic Practice, Pragmatic Vistas

Louise Rosenblatt and the Reader's Response

For anyone old enough to have been a student before the midcentury mark, one of the pleasures of reading Louise Rosenblatt is encountering old friends—interesting minor figures like Maud Bodkin, Rosamond Lehmann, and Gordon Allport, as well as giants like John Dewey, Franz Boas, and Edward Sapir. It is not a matter of nostalgia but of recalling a time when the philosophy of education was more concerned with ideas than with data. It is inspiriting to read Louise Rosenblatt, because her conviction that critical theory and classroom practice are philosophical to the core is voiced on every page. For younger readers, one of the chief benefits is to be set straight about certain events and movements and schools which have been in recent times badly misunderstood and wantonly misrepresented. She was one of the first to recognize the significance of I. A. Richards' *Practical Criticism*, to understand what the purposes of the New Criticism were and how certain of the proponents of this critical practice derailed the enterprise. For all readers, there is the pleasure of reading straightforward prose about the importance of literature in our lives and the logical, psychological, pedagogical, and political reasons for beginning with the reader's response.

First published in the special issue on Louise M. Rosenblatt, *Reader*, 20 (Fall, 1988).

Defining the context for Rosenblatt's theory of the reader's role takes us to the heart of American philosophy. It would be salutary for contemporary critics to turn to her explanation of her principal ideas because they will find there a more authentic understanding of Peirce and James than they will get, say, in reading one American academic's interpretation of another's redaction of a British expositor's rendition of an idea gleaned from a European critic's uninstructed reading of Peirce. Sometimes cross-cultural exchange can be generative, as when Martin Luther King, Jr. found in Gandhi what Gandhi had taken from Thoreau, who had gathered it, in part, from Eastern mysticism. But the reheated, refiltered, decaffeinated criticism currently available is neither generative nor instructive. Reading Rosenblatt brings us closer to the genuine sources of some of the most significant concepts in contemporary philosophy.

I want to claim that Rosenblatt exemplifies pragmatism at its best. The student of John Dewey and a careful reader of William James, she is attentive to both logical and psychological dimensions of theory and practice. Further, she is at home with what I. A. Richards called Peirce's "revolutionary doctrine of the Interpretant." The Interpretant is the idea that mediates the symbol and its referent; it is part of the sign, an element of the meaning relationship. It is held, generally speaking, by an individual person, but Peirce was very reluctant, except as "a Sop to Cerberus," to conflate the person and the idea because he did not want to lose the point that interpretation is logically constitutive and not a psychological additive. In Peirce's semiotics (he invented the term, which he spelled *semeiotic*), the meaning relationship is three-valued, triadic: interpretation is entailed in signification. Saussure's signifier-signified, in contrast, is two-valued, with interpretation seen as a psychological additive. Modern linguistics derives from Saussure and tends to be centrally concerned with neither meaning nor interpretation. Understanding the two varieties of semiotics is crucial to understanding how and why Rosenblatt's theories differ from other varieties of what is generally called "reader-response" theory.

Naming the theory which holds that the reader's response is important in many different senses is not easy: "reader response" is slightly pleonastic, for from where else would there be a response? But, of course, the point is not what phrase we decide on but what we mean by it. A pragmatic understanding takes active, interpretive practice as the chief consequence of triadicity: if all knowledge is mediated, then we must continually interpret our interpretations. If there is no direct access to reality, truth, or any other absolute, then we must look to our practice to mediate our understanding. If we apply the pragmatic maxim—what difference would it make to our practice if we hold thus and so?—the advantages are immediately apparent. For the pedagogical implications of reader-response theory are very rich indeed and it is for her careful exploration of them that we have chiefly to thank Rosenblatt. Three distinctions provide points of departure for that exploration: interaction/transaction, text/poem, efferent/aesthetic. In all cases, a triadic conception supplants a dyadic one: transaction, poem, aesthetic stance are, in Rosenblatt's hands, thoroughly triadic, thoroughly pragmatic. I will consider them in the order named.

Transaction, Rosenblatt explains, is Dewey's term, a concept he meant to supplant the idea of interaction, which was modeled on the stimulus-response of behavioral psychology. For Dewey the organism in its environment was, like the sign, a three-valued relationship. Nowadays, the notions of recursion and feedback are familiar from information theory, the role it plays in our computer-driven lives, but the complexity of what Rosenblatt, following Gregory Bateson, calls "ecological naturalism" is still not widely recognized. Any and all ideas can be reduced to dyadic terms, with the result that generative power is lost; that is to say, transaction will be nothing but interaction if it is entertained in the dyadic perspective, as a matter of I'll-scratch-your-back-if-you'll-scratch-mine.[1] Transaction, as Rosenblatt intends it, means that the relationship between the reader and what he reads is not dyadic, like stimulus-response, but is mediated by what he brings to what he reads, by what he presupposes and analyzes and conjectures and concludes about what is being said and what it might mean. *Transaction* is meant to keep the dialectic apparent and lively, but of course the word alone cannot do that: we must form the concept, and to do so we will need concepts to think with, chief among them experience.

Rosenblatt's argument for the primacy of experience is important for us, remembering how this idea has fared in educational philosophy. I would say that underlying her conception of experience is Boas's and Sapir's understanding of language as at once a formal system and a means of cultural and individual expression. Experience, that is to say, is never "merely personal," and its social character is defining. It isn't enough to say "personal experience" any more than it is to say that interpretation is what an interpreter does; *experience* and *person* must both be defined in terms of our social existence. This understanding is best modeled by language seen as a species-specific capacity which can be realized only in the context of our lives as social creatures. Piaget's structuralism hid this truth from view, though recent study of Vygotsky has helped to reclaim it. But Rosenblatt does not let us forget the dialectic:

> To affirm that the individual consciousness embodies forces that transcend the biological organism, that there is no sharp division between the subjective consciousness and its object does not require dispensing with the vital, dynamic, active, empirical self. (*The Reader, The Text and The Poem* 172).

The self is, she contends, not a "construct," but neither is it an autonomous entity. This is consonant with what Peirce meant in saying that Man is a Sign: he is Thirdness to the facts of the Universe.

Experience is always social and it is active: it is not a collection of responses to a collection of stimuli. Experience is, for one thing, the memory of acts and events, represented in images of all sorts. The fact that Rosenblatt draws upon the Ames perception studies is evidence that she has seen how "the prime agent of all human perception"—Coleridge's famous definition of Imagination—is active and creative. Along with an anthropologically sophisticated understanding of language, there is a theory of imagination which underwrites her reader-response theory; indeed, her theory could be said to bear about the same relationship to "affective stylistics" and "subjective criticism" as Imagination does to Fancy.

In calling the experience of reading a *transaction*, Rosenblatt is recognizing interpretation as a process of making meaning. It is a nonlinear, dynamic, dialectical process in which we continually interpret our interpretations. Response really begins not with the "response" but with the student's reflection on the response. Her thoroughly pragmatic sense of what is "valid" in a reading puts the emphasis on seeing what difference taking part of a text *this* way would make to the rest of it. This critical respect for how the reading of one line or image or passage will necessarily affect the way we read other elements of the text is an expression of the same principle which guides Richards in his insistence on the possibility of distinguishing "variant readings" from "misreading" (see p. 112). Thus, Rosenblatt and Richards share an understanding of recognizing, identifying, and evaluating textual constraints on the reader's response: they both follow the pragmatic maxim. Solipsists should take notice—and those for whom the vague notion of an "interpretive community" has supplanted the well-formed concept of transaction.

If there is a drawback to the term *transaction*—and I think there is—it is that it reifies the text, suggesting a power and position equal to that of the reader. Like the more up-to-date term *negotiate*, it implies two parties of equal status. Now, it may be that the reader and the writer have this relationship, but the author is not in the picture in reader-response models. To see the transaction as taking place between a gabby reader and a gabby text always reminds me, rather, of the stomach talking to its owner, the thoughtless consumer of pepperoni pizzas in the Alka Selzer ad. The opposition of reader and text as copartners in a transaction represents a dyadic semiotics. The transaction is actually between varying interpretations, starts and stops, as they are constrained by an ever-deepening appreciation of the limits of language represented in the text, in dialectic with the experience the reader brings to the reading. Rosenblatt's emphasis on this interdependency of openness and reflection reminds us that her hermeneutics, like her semiotics, is triadic and pragmatic. Awareness of this can protect us from misconceiving what *transaction* is meant to express.

Just so, in her differentiation of *text* and *poem*, Rosenblatt is mindful of what Richards calls "the problem of initial terms." Rather than speaking of a text as "essentially" or "actually" or "really" traces of graphite on processed pulp, or some such circumlocution, Rosenblatt begins with symbols:

> "Text" designates a set or series of signs interpretable as linguistic symbols. I use this rather roundabout phrasing to make it clear that the text is not simply the inked marks on the page or even the uttered vibrations in the air. The visual or auditory signs become verbal symbols, become words, by virtue of their being potentially recognizable as pointing to something beyond themselves. Thus, in a reading situation "the text" may be thought of as the printed signs in their capacity to serve as symbols (*The Reader, The Text and the Poem* 12).

And when we recreate the text as poem, those verbal symbols are interpreted, their meanings construed. For this reason, a theory of reading must have a working concept of discourse as well as a philosophy of language: words and letters are not the initial terms of discourse; meanings are.

It has been a chief contribution of hermeneutics to shift the focus of critical theory from abstract definitions of discourse to the nature of the reading process, from rhetoric to interpretation, if you will. Schleiermacher, generally credited by those who chart intellectual currents as the founder of a general theory of hermeneutics, held that we construct the text by means of a "grammatical" approach, but that to penetrate to the inner form, we must rely on the "divinatory" power. And he meant nothing mystical: this power is ours by virtue of our common human experience. It seems to me that Rosenblatt is instructive and inspiriting when she is discussing the transactional stance, which entails just such a dialectical method; but when she turns to what purports to be two kinds of reading, one is less certain of their relationship.

In the case of this pair, *efferent/aesthetic*, by the time Rosenblatt has explained how both can play a role in reading either literature or mathematical formulas, one might wonder if they are worth keeping. *Efferent* sounds too close to *reading out*, which with *reading in* constitutes a pernicious dichotomy. The notion that first we neutrally decode the words on the page and then we respond is at odds with Rosenblatt's teaching, but the term *efferent* rather distracts us (me?) from her sense that the reader responds from first to last in terms of his experience. For Rosenblatt, the reader responds by means of the meanings which emerge in the process of reading. Taken with *aesthetic*, *efferent* might suggest, in the absence of a triadic conception of the sign, that meaning making is being deferred. If we remember, however, that *efferent* and *aesthetic* are meant to be taken together, that it is a matter not of sequence but of focus, these terms can serve us in our thinking about the reader's response.

Two other pairs of terms can illuminate Rosenblatt's distinctive pair. One is Wolfgang Iser's *wandering eye/focus*. Mariolina Salvatori has given us an excellent explication of this concept and has noted the pedagogical implications.[2] And I hope someone will investigate Rosenblatt's distinction in the light of C.S. Lewis's between *use* and *receive*.[3] Iser's pair opposes mutually dependent activities; Lewis's are mutually exclusive. We are asked to renounce "use"—reading for message or comfort—and to cultivate instead the habit of receiving what literature has to offer.

One source of confusion is, I think, that Rosenblatt's pair sometimes functions like Iser's and sometimes like Lewis's, but it's what she does with her concepts that counts. Her conception of the aesthetic stance guides her in a brilliant critique of E. D. Hirsch's attempt to deploy Frege's *Sinn* (significance or import) and *Bedeutung* (referent) for purposes which, as she explains, Frege excluded. All philosophers must make a stab at differentiating not only what-is-said and what-is-meant but also the modes of representing both what-is-said and what-is-meant. Frege knew that the relationship of these two aspects in works of art is not of the same sort as that relationship in scientific statement. What Richards wrestled with for forty years; what Wittgenstein despaired of figuring out, counseling silence at the end of the *Tractatus*; what Susanne K. Langer labored to develop, a philosophy of presentational form: what others have seen as one of the most challenging philosophical problems of the twentieth century Hirsch meets by muddling and misapplying terms. Rosenblatt provides as good protection as anyone I have read against Hirsch's theory of authorial intention, which he identifies with Frege's *Bedeutung*.

There are other gangster theories which she can help us defend ourselves against, such as that "structuralist poetics" which sets meaning aside in order to study the codes and conventions that make meaning possible or that deconstruction which Paul de Man proclaims as the mission of literary study in years to come, the collapse of poem into text. Getting rid of the interpreter or destroying what he is meant to interpret are variants of a view of language as a substitute for reality and of literature as only self-referential. As she discusses the actualities of reading, it is clear that Rosenblatt begins, as Vygotsky advises, with "the unit of meaning" and that she suffers from no irrational anxiety about the impossibility of ever knowing what is meant directly, by revelation or no-fault decoding.

Rosenblatt's theory of reading is, like Freire's pedagogy of knowing and Richards' philosophy of rhetoric, informed by a trust in what Coleridge called "the all-in-each of human nature." And because of the way she conceives of language and literature, learning to read is the means of learning virtue:

> When we are helping students to better techniques of reading through greater sensitivity to diction, tone, structure, image, symbol, narrative movement, we are also helping them to make the more refined responses that are ultimately the source of human understanding and sensitivity to human values (*Literature as Exploration* 290).

With Rosenblatt as our guide, we will recognize and celebrate the social contexts of literature, confident that her theory of literature will protect us from "using" it, from teaching for message.

I began by claiming that Rosenblatt is a thoroughgoing pragmatist and that that is why we have from her such sound guidance for our practice. Her trust in the power of the mind; her commitment to honest and open questioning and discussion; her understanding of the political importance of learning to tolerate not only other people's opinions but ambiguity itself: these are, of course, not exclusively American traits, but when they are found in conjunction with belief in democratic values, we certainly want to claim them as American. Rosenblatt closed one book with John Keats and the other with Walt Whitman—and that makes the symbolic point: her love of beauty is joined by her teacher's passion for literature as exploration, as the best way to open up democratic vistas. In her important essay, "Whitman's Democratic Vistas and the New 'Ethnicity,' " she shows us how responsive reading—authentic interpretation—reclaims the hermeneutic bond of individual and community, what Schleiermacher saw as the way each person represents humanity in his own way. She writes:

> Whitman enjoins upon us an active selectivity, a testing, a rejection of all derived from an ancestry that is alien to the special needs of a free society. . . . Whitman shows us the man and woman accepting themselves in all their uniqueness, honoring their own roots, but free to reach out in all directions to their fellow humans (199–200).

Louise Rosenblatt makes me proud to be an American.

Notes

1. For Father Ong, transaction is only an ongoing interaction. This profoundly positivist conception trips him into contradiction: "An

interpretation," he writes, "is shaped by the text as a given reader interacted with it" ("Beyond Objectivity: The Reader-Writer Transaction as an Altered State of Consciousness," *The CEA Critic,* 40 (1977), 6–13). A few sentences later we find him saying that "a text reacts not at all to any interpretation." The second statement is clearly true, if you remove the text from any dialectical relationship with emergent discourse, and it negates the first statement, since interaction surely entails reaction.

2. Mariolina Salvatori, "The Pedagogical Implications of Reader-Response Theory," *Reader,* 16 (1986), 1–19.

3. See *An Experiment in Criticism* (Cambridge: Cambridge University Press, 1961). Here is one of Lewis's explanations: "A work of (whatever) art can be either 'received' or 'used.' When we receive it we exert our senses and imagination and various other powers according to a pattern invented by the artist. When we 'use' it we treat it as an assistance for our own activities. The one, to use an old-fashioned image, is like being taken for a bicycle ride by a man who may know roads we have never yet explored. The other is like adding one of those motor attachments to our own bicycle and then going for one of our familiar rides. These rides may in themselves be good, bad, or indifferent. . . . 'Using' is inferior to 'reception' because art, if used rather than received, merely facilitates, brightens, relieves, or palliates our life, and does not add to it" (88).

11

I. A. Richards and the Concept of Literacy

I. A. Richards was neither a rhetorician nor a linguist, but he wrote continually about the philosophy of rhetoric and the science of signs. From first to last, he was a great teacher—one of the greatest of this century, I would say, in the class with Maria Montessori, Jane Addams, Paulo Freire, and any others who simultaneously have defined a field and a method. And for all his incorrigible Britishness, Richards was a world citizen. His hope was to help build an orderly, humane society; to help imagine a peaceful world. When he went to China in 1930, it was because he believed that when China came to enter the modern era, we of the West should be able to recognize what we had to learn from the Chinese. His aim was to find the Chinese Plato, and when he had found him—it was Mencius —what he wrote was, typically, not a disquisition on Mencius's ideas but an essay on what would be needed if we were to think as Mencius did. He developed translation as a model for critical inquiry, including demonstrations of how multiple definition could enable us to maintain a lively dialectic between what is said and what is meant.

Richards was a literary critic of great distinction, but that, as Chekhov would say, is a tune from a different opera. For our

---

Read, in a somewhat different form, at the Conference on Literary Criticism and Literacy, University of San Francisco, June 1988.

purposes, his most important contribution came in a role he invented, performing as what we might today call a teacher researcher. In *Practical Criticism*, Richards demonstrated that when students at Cambridge University were confronted with untitled poems, the authors unidentified, they did not know how to read for sense and meaning and fell back on stock responses and other tricks. Richards was the first critic—have there been others?—to take student writing as texts which required interpretation. The protocols which participants in this experiment submitted were analyzed with as much care as he expended on Swinburne and Shelley, Shakespeare and Donne.

The effect of *Practical Criticism* was dramatic: it gave English studies a reason for being and helped recruit teachers for decades. By offering techniques of close reading as an alternative to the "appreciation" which was bidding to succeed the old philology, this book became one of the founding charters of the New Criticism. But that is not to say that Richards' program was found interesting or instructive; indeed, it has been largely ignored. I believe we could see a new day if the Introduction and Summary of *Practical Criticism* were required reading in every graduate seminar in rhetoric and composition. For one thing, they offer excellent protection against what Richards elsewhere called "gangster theories." And a great deal could be learned about the aims and the limitations of research design. Richards keeps the particular problems revealed by the protocols in dialectic with his larger concerns, as in this passage:

> The deficiencies so noticeable in the protocol writers . . . are not native inalterable defects in the average human mind. They are due in a large degree to mistakes that can be avoided and to bad training. In fact, does anyone ever receive any useful training in this matter? Yet, without asking more from average humanity than even a misanthrope will grant something can be done to make men's spiritual heritage more available and more operative (*Practical Criticism* 291).

I would be surprised to learn that the word *spirit* or anything we might mean by it has ever appeared in *Research in the Teaching of English* or *Studies in Writing and Rhetoric*.

Richards had reclaimed the phrase "practical criticism"

from Coleridge, and it was Coleridge, he was fond of saying, who led him "from criticism to creation," which is the way he thought of education. Beginning with *Mencius on the Mind*, Richards draws out the implications of what *Practical Criticism* had demonstrated. What was called for was a new and different way of teaching reading, but whereas he had declared in *Practical Criticism* that psychology was the indispensable instrument, he soon came to see that psychology was inadequate and that only philosophy could guide the inquiry he had now begun to conduct. Seven years after *Practical Criticism*, there appeared *The Philosophy of Rhetoric*. Everyone who declares emancipation from Aristotle calls his salvation a "new rhetoric" and Richards was no different. The new rhetoric for which he called in 1936 would "take charge of the criticism of its assumptions"—a challenge which most rhetoricians have yet to harken to, so busy are they with their taxonomies. Richards' new rhetoric was to focus not on the so-called modes of discourse but on language; rhetoric he called a "study of how words work," which is what he and Ogden had said of their science of signs, in *The Meaning of Meaning*.

Richards held that the best place to start with a study of how words work was with misunderstandings and their remedies. It is a point of greatest interest that everything comes together here: rhetoric is identified as an inquiry which must be guided by a semiotics, and it is identified as a hermeneutic enterprise. The idea that we begin with misunderstandings is precisely the premise Schleiermacher defends in explaining the character of a general theory of hermeneutics, the art and science of interpretation. Adding that we should attend to remedies is testimony to Richards' pragmatism, his insistence that no theory is worth its salt if we can't determine what difference it would make to our practice. Now, remediation has somehow gotten a bad name in composition theory and practice. The sentimental positivism which typifies so much current rhetorical theory insists that we should reject the idea of remediation because it suggests pathology. Of course, it is wrongheaded to treat error, misconception, ignorance, and incompetence as moral failures or as matters of personal blame, but that attitude should not extend to a rejection of the idea of diagnosis. Student failures must be recognized, diagnosed, and treated. Medicine, like law and exegesis, is one of the original hermeneutic arts, as sport, be it noted, is not. The notion of language games, the metaphor of teachers as coaches, of

teaching as an intervention by an umpire are all far more hazardous than medical metaphors of diagnosis and remedy.

Richards was so far ahead of his time that we haven't
caught up with him yet. The best way to do so, in my view,
is to consider his critique of modern linguistics. As he turned
from psychology to the philosophy of rhetoric, he quickly saw
that the science of signs, as it was developing in modern linguistics, was not only beside the point but dangerously mis-
conceived. He continually reminded his readers (who were
becoming fewer and fewer) that information theory was illog-
ically deployed by psycholinguistics and was irrelevant for the
study of discourse. He patiently explained that the Morse Code
and a code of etiquette are not of the same sort. He argued
carefully and substantially that signal and message should not
be confused, that what is encoded and decoded is signal and
that messages are generated by contexts and are dependent not
only on the interpretation of the code but on the interpretation
of what is said. When Jonathan Culler, following Todorov, declares with an arrogance all his own that a structuralist poetics
is concerned not with meaning but with "the codes and conventions which make meaning possible," he has forgotten the
central principle of semiotics (if he ever knew it), that it is only
by means of meanings that we are able to apprehend meaning,
or to create new meanings.

Every writing teacher has read or has been influenced by
Roman Jakobson's famous "Closing Statement" at a conference
on style held in 1958 in which he set forth his conception of
"the communication situation." Richards problematized this
presentation many times, most importantly in an essay entitled
"Towards a Theory of Comprehending" (*Reclaiming* 172–186),
but this critique remains unacknowledged by those who need
it. Nor is it remembered that Richards contributed two papers
at that same conference. One was entitled "Variant Readings
and Misreading." The climate in which such a pedagogical
concern could be entertained was not to come for another twenty-
five years or so. Meanwhile, we have had the apotheosis of
misreading, the spurious conception of "interpretive commu-
nities," the absurdities of "subjective" criticism, and other debased forms of reader-response theory. We have had affective
stylistics and, worst of all, the mystifications of deconstruction. When Paul de Man declared that semiology abrogated the
need for interpretation because "the linguistic elements themselves" reveal the code, he was proudly staking out territory

as far removed from Richards' principles as it is possible to get and, I would claim, as far from the authentic concerns of English teachers, literary critics, readers, and writers as it is possible to get.

My dyspeptic contention is this: current critical theory (which does not condescend to concern itself with pedagogy) is entirely irrelevant to our enterprise, insofar as we are interested in teaching students to read critically, to think cogently, and to write coherently. Insofar as we are concerned with the problems and issues of literacy and illiteracy, we will find no guidance from what Frederick Crews has called The Grand Academy of Theory. Even worse is the pretentious and wrong-headed advice offered by those who consider themselves at war with the Grand Academy. The very idea of *cultural literacy* is a case in point. The form of E. D. Hirsch's title is a symptom of positivist thinking; indeed, any such modification of *literacy* reduces the meaning of that word to *decoding*. If we speak of *cultural* literacy, we mean decoding skills plus interpretation —a positivist conception underwritten by the dyadic sign. Hirsch, you may remember, argued several years ago that teaching composition would be a snap if we addressed ourselves to subskills, among which he listed *organization*, right next to *punctuation*. When this didn't pan out, he announced with great humility that he'd been wrong and that subskills couldn't be learned unless students knew what they were needed for. So far, so good, but Professor Hirsch is no teacher; he hasn't a pedagogical bone in his body. His response was not to change his conception of what or how to teach. His response, with *Cultural Literacy*, has been to say to the schools: "Get them ready for me so that I can lecture on Wordsworth without having to stop to explain what a daffodil is or the meaning of *diurnal*. Teach them the subskills, of course, but don't forget The Facts."

When we qualify *literacy—cultural* literacy, *functional* literacy, or (God save us) *essayistic* literacy—the logical result of all such modification is to reduce *literacy* to meaning the code or the medium or the graphic representation alone. Now, the essential point is that the necessary and sufficient conditions are interdependent: there is no authentic literacy if it does not serve the making of meaning. If we insist on taking literacy to mean essentially the mastery of a code, we should remember that this is the kind of learning which chimps and rats can manage. If we assume that this allegedly essential coding activity comes *first*, then the way is open for drill and workbooks and all the techniques of education conceived of as banking or alimentation, as Freire has it. If we dichotomize the making of meaning and the graphic representation of meaning, we will have a very hard time ever getting them together. The failure to apprehend the logic of the sufficient and necessary conditions of literacy leads directly to a confusion which has very dangerous political implications. If we hold that literacy essentially means construing and constructing letters, without regard for meaning, we will be unable to understand why becoming literate, in this sense, has no necessary consequences. If *meaning* is reduced to meaning graphic codes, without accounting for social contexts and cultural frameworks, then we shouldn't be surprised when this so-called literacy turns out to have no social significance or political consequences. Freire was not sent into exile because he was teaching *ba-be-bi-bo-bu*. His government (and don't ever forget that your government and mine aided and abetted the government of Brazil: the CIA burned his primers and smashed his slide projectors) feared him because literacy for Freire entails the development of critical consciousness.

Along with Freire, I think we can usefully turn to Vygotsky for guidance in this matter of understanding the logic of literacy. Vygotsky argued that the dialectic of thought and language could not be apprehended by beginning with one and adding the other. On the model of the living cell, he explained that we must begin with "the unit of meaning." I have been claiming that literacy must be apprehended not as a signal code-plus-message but as a unity, as the representation of meaning.

In any case, definition of *literacy* is not all we need. Rhetoricians and composition specialists and educationists all have a bad habit—it's a positivist tic—of letting lexical definition do the job of conceptualizing. They organize conferences around questions like "What IS English?" "What IS rhetoric?" "What IS literacy?" The alternative is to transform a definition by means of the pragmatic maxim. Pragmatism doesn't mean asking "Does it work?" or "How much will it cost?" or "Can we get away with it?" The pragmatist—the Peircean pragmaticist—asks: "If we put it this way, what difference will it make to our practice?" I offer a definition of literacy which I will first problematize—interpreting it as an interpretation—and then transform by means of the pragmatic maxim.

I have always admired the third grader's mode of definition: "Taxation is when they take your money." Kenneth Burke remarks that names are "titles for situations," and the third grader here is transforming the name to a situation. On this model, we could say "Literacy is when you can read and write meaningfully." Here's an interpretive paraphrase of that definition: "Literacy is the realized capacity to construct and construe in graphic form representations of our recognitions."

Realized capacity *Realize* is here used in the French sense of being made manifest, expressed. I avoid the term *competence* because certain literary theorists have thoroughly muddled it by speaking of *"literary* competence." By *capacity* I mean the species-specific power of symbolization. Indeed, my definition of *literacy* is actually modeled on Sapir's definition of language as "the vocal actualization of the tendency to see reality symbolically."

Construct and **construe** These "mentalistic" terms for *writing* and *reading* are intended as a rhetorical defense against the gangster theory that language is "verbal behavior," or that thinking is properly to be called "human information processing." Constructing and construing are acts of mind; they are interpretive and heuristic; they are hermeneutic operations. I hold with Susanne K. Langer that "all knowledge is interpretation," remembering that all interpretation is subject to interpretation, necessarily.

Graphic form I have noted that the code—the signal, what is represented in graphic form—is the necessary condition, not the sufficient condition for literacy. Without it, literacy quickly becomes a pseudo-concept in Vygotsky's sense—a catchall with no means of differentiating all that is caught. Literacy should not be made to mean "coping skills"—and "oral literacy" is an oxymoron. But, again, literacy must not be identified with the graphic form itself: *write it down* is not the same as *write it up.*

Representation This word must be reclaimed as the name for a vitally important concept which certain positivists calling themselves "Neo-pragmatists" are trying to stamp out. They take *representation* to mean copying and since we all know that language or any other symbolic form does not simply copy, they get away with saying that no form can "represent." We need a triadic understanding of representation; that is to say, we need to see it as always the representation of a representation. (Positivists detest those circularities; Richards loved them and made them up continually.) Representation, seen in triadic terms, is mediation—the means of making meaning.

Recognition The secret of the universe is that recognition comes before cognition; recognition is the logical condition of cognition. We don't just *see*; we always *see as*. What we need is not more cognitive scientists in white coats, muddling all the terms of critical discourse; we need *recognition* scientists—teachers!

Now here's the transform: "If we hold the idea that literacy is *the realized capacity to construct and construe in graphic form representations of our recognitions*, what difference would it make to our practice?" I want to answer that question by referring to Richards' theory and practice, taking the terms of my working definition in reverse order, from *recognition* to *representation, graphic form, construct and construe*, and ending with *literacy*.

Recognition, like imagination, is generally discussed in terms of visual perception. Richards believed that "modes of intellectual energy"—a phrase he quotes from Coleridge—can be discovered best in the process of "learning and looking." In his idiosyncratic use of information theory, Richards held that two channels are better than one and that looking at texts while we listen to them being read is excellent practice in those acts of mind which interpretation requires. He used the word *notation* to name the means by which we apprehend and record our recognitions: they are audio, visual, and graphic. And, though I don't think he ever wrote about it, he certainly included kinesis as a mode of notation. As a champion mountaineer, he had certain extraordinary subskills: he could jump straight up from the floor to a height of three feet or so and would do just that, leaping on to the desktop to illustrate a metrical point. One of his former T. A.s has told me about the job he had in the days when Richards was going around to high schools in the 1950s. Richards would read from his translation of *The Iliad* in Basic English, but he would first read in Greek. The T. A. would tie one end of a jump rope to the radiator and turn it, in accompaniment to Richards' reading: this kinetic notation represented the Aegean Sea pounding the shore.

Representation to Richards meant symbolization. Peirce held that logic itself is "the philosophy of representation" and Richards followed him in insisting pragmatically that theory be represented in actual demonstrations and depicted, wherever possible, in diagrams. In explaining the use of multiple definitions, Richards wrote in *Mencius on the Mind* that "unless we actually and constantly sketch out alternative definitions using different logical machinery we shall not gain the ability to experiment in interpretation which comparative studies require." All that we know is mediated—represented—and must therefore be interpreted. The chief pedagogical consequence of triadicity for Richards was this concept of experimentation and it was for that reason that he called the classroom a "philosophic laboratory" in which the object of study was the relationship of what is said and what is meant. The speculative instruments for such study were to be the meanings represented in our interpretations. Although he speaks of "logical machinery" here, in 1932, before long he turned to organic metaphors and to the conception of instruments instead of tools.

Richards stressed the role of graphic form in the representation of our recognitions. Both words and pictures were used in the primers he developed with Christine Gibson, *English Through Pictures, Spanish Through Pictures*, etc. Depictions presented the oppositional pairs in one channel; the text, prepared according to the principles of Basic English and meant to be read aloud, did so in another channel. *The hat is here./ The hat is there.* Near/big and far/little became the means of representing the meaning of *here/there*, the difference between them; and the repetition of *hat* and *is* represents sameness. To ascertain what varies with what Richards considered the aim and method of all critical inquiry.

Richards was convinced that television would make literacy training feasible for the entire planet because it would activate the natural capacity of recognition. He was fond of comparing the emergence from the Homeric world to the literate age with the advent of electronic means of recording our representations of recognitions. "The question is," he wrote, "whether the new or restored opportunities now offered to speech, when superimposed on the established techniques of reading and writing, can work the miracle again." He was convinced that they could.

The relationship of constructing and construing to graphic form is at the heart of the current debate over the relationship of literacy to cognition. Richards' work alerts us to what he calls "the problem of initial terms." If we take literacy to mean decoding, or if we limit it to the simplest functions of language, then it will be logically impossible to define any necessary relationship of literacy to the development of conceptual power.

If, on the other hand, we take literacy to be the power of representing in graphic form, if we keep coding and codification together (to call on Freire's terminology), we can then see more clearly what we are doing in teaching reading and writing. For Richards, they are decidedly *not* just technologies:

> So long as we suppose that writing merely replaces possible speech, takes care only of the absence of the audience, for example, we won't at all understand what it can do for us (*The Written Word* 68).

No wonder reading experts are so enamored of the concept of "decontextualism": it allows them to hold on to the ladder of abstraction, the most venerable of positivist tools! I don't think Richards would have been surprised to hear a psycholinguist announce recently that reading and writing are supererogatory, that they will soon be classified with other archaic activities like quiltmaking. For Richards, the techniques (not, be it noted, "technologies") of reading and writing do indeed bring about a change in the power of mind. He speaks of the preliterate mind and "the writing mind," and he has no pastoral fondness for the oral tradition, though he is quick to point out that Socrates, who invented both philosophy and the Soul, never *wrote* anything. But what happens with literacy to empower the mind?

> With written language, [the learner] gains means of exploring and comparing he never had before. . . . Visual notation compels us to attend severally to the parts (of an utterance) themselves and yet connectedly to their places within a whole (*The Written Word* 67).

Those dry sentences appear in an essay written forty years after *Mencius on the Mind*. They are worth more than thousands and thousands of pages by experts for whom literacy means a behavioral response to signals. They are followed by a somewhat more passionate statement. Richards has been noting the dangers of "the guessing game" and urging instead learning to see "composedly" rather than with bewilderment. He writes:

> Children should be working at reading not just to learn to read, not even just to enjoy stories, still less to be able to spell and pronounce correctly, and certainly not just to

get jobs—but to develop further their distinctive quality as human beings: intelligent, self-corrigible discernment (*The Written Word* 81).

To Terry Eagleton and his ilk, the idea of "self-corrigible discernment" would probably sound like a preppy obsession: "How can I answer on my orals so I'm sure to get a Summa?" For the positivist, the self is merely personal, merely private, a merely psychological entity. In triadic terms, the self is the center (and that does not mean "self-centeredness"); "self-corrigible discernment," as it is a distinctive human quality, is what Peirce meant by "the sense of learning." It is the power of reflection, the power of interpreting our interpretations, the power of self-knowledge. Here is Richards commenting on this process of coming to know our knowledge:

> Any utterance may be regarded as a moment in a continuing series of interpretants . . . , an endless development endeavoring to correct itself (*Design for Escape* 45).

Correction—the effect of being corrigible—is the motive power of interpretation.

In terms of Peirce's triadic conception of the sign, the self is not isolated and its correcting discernment goes on in social contexts—necessarily. Each sign, Peirce held, requires another for its interpretation; further, he held that Man is a Sign. Take these two premises together and you have the logic of what is now being called "the social construction of knowledge," what Peirce called "synechism." Each Man-Sign requires other Man-Signs in order to interpret his interpretations: it is only as we see it reflected in the interpretations of others that we can come to know our knowledge. Thus "self-corrigible discernment" is not a private, psychological behavior but a social, semiotic activity.

Richards learned from Peirce how to think triadically; he never forgot the Third. From Coleridge he learned to think of language as "the supreme organ of the mind's self-ordering growth." Every time he writes *mind* or *self*, we should read "the all-in-each of human nature," Coleridge's wonderful name for the special powers which belong to all of us and which are realized socially, communally. They are assured by reason of language and imagination, species-specific powers which are, in turn, the means of assuring those inalienable rights with which we are endowed by our Creator. In the epistemology of Romanticism, the self is no solitary entity. Thus, Schleiermacher, friend of Herder, discoverer of feeling as the wellspring of metaphysics, declared that his "highest intuition" was that "each man represents humanity in his own way." This is not a utopian fantasy, nor is it a gender issue: *Representative Man* is an invention of the typological imagination, a creation which we English teachers must, I think, continually reinvent, identifying the generic resonance in "Man."

Richards' language derives from Romanticism, but his theory and practice are, I believe, entirely consonant with Freire's. Both know how to think about thinking. Both would know that *praxis* is both action and reflection, that *practical criticism* is at once theoretical and actual. Where Richards speaks of *self* and *mind*, Freire speaks of *subject* and *consciousness*; what Richards calls *speculative instruments*, Freire calls *generative words*. Freire's *problematizing the existential situation* is a matter of reading the world with precisely the same attitude as that with which Richards reads texts: ambiguities are for him "the very hinges of all thought" and he locates them by a process of problem posing. What Freire calls "the banking concept of education" Richards, with quite the same sense of the danger, calls "psittacism." For Richards, thinking is a matter of "comprehending our comprehensions more comprehensively"; for Freire, it is "consciousness as consciousness of consciousness, intent upon the world" (*The Pedagogy of the Oppressed* 66). For both great teachers, pedagogy is rooted in the sense of community, in dialogue, in activity. For Richards and Freire, language is social, and the self—the knowing subject—is the agency of our humanity. Listen to the revolutionary hermeneutic each announces in his own way:

> Banking education inhibits creativity and domesticates (although it cannot completely destroy) the intentionality of consciousness by isolating consciousness from the world, thereby denying men their ontological and historical vocation of becoming more human. Problem-posing education bases itself on creativity and stimulates true reflection and action upon reality, thereby responding to the vocation of men as beings who are authentic only when engaged in inquiry and creative transformation. . . . Banking theory and practice, as immobilizing and fixating forces, fail to acknowledge men as historical beings; prob-

lem-posing theory and practice take man's historicity as their starting point (*The Pedagogy of the Oppressed* 71).

A discussion of the reasons for the choice of words— which too often seems a trivial exchange of whimsies— can become an introduction to the theory of all choices. The art of so transforming it from a tea-table topic into the central discipline of education waits to be rediscovered, but the better we understand what place words hold in our lives the readier we shall be to admit that to think about their choice is the most convenient mode of thinking about the principle of all our choices (*The Philosophy of Rhetoric* 81).

And who wrote this?

With the formula we think we have the essence, the BEING, of the thing, caught in a holdfast of thoughts or words. But there are no holdfasts in philosophy. The knowledge we seek is not something we should hope to HAVE, as something separate from a power to understand. Insofar as we come to know the form—as opposed to a formula —of a thing, we become able to see the why of what it does and undergoes. To see this is to take into our minds the forms of things we understand, knowing them by becoming them. . . . Knowledge in seeking form must not leave the world behind it. When it does, it arrives in a mere ghost world of words. The great disease of knowledge is that in which, starting from words, we end up with them.

And this?

As we attempt to analyze dialogue as a human phenomenon, we discover something which is the essence of dialogue itself: *the word*. But the word is more than just an instrument which makes dialogue possible; accordingly, we must seek its constitutive elements. Within the word we find two dimensions, reflection and action, in such radical interaction that if one is sacrificed—even in part —the other immediately suffers. There is no true word that is not at the same time a praxis. Thus to speak a true word is to transform the world.

The sense of learning and the pedagogy of knowing arise from one and the same source, the recognition that all knowledge is interpretation, that interpretation is the work of the active mind. Richards, like Freire, can guide our understanding of literacy as the mind in action, re-creating, correcting, interpreting, transforming the self and society. Has any other profession so high a calling as ours?

Epilogue

Ramus Meets Schleiermacher and They Go Off for a Triadic Lunch with Peirce; Vico Drops By

This imaginary conversation is *not* offered as a contribution to the conversation of mankind. It is *not* modeled on Terry Eagleton's novel, recently published, in which Wittgenstein's brother discusses critical theory with those assembled in an Irish country house (I find everything about Terry Eagleton uncongenial, except his occasional wit). I have never read Walter Savage Landor's *Imaginary Conversations*, so I shouldn't steal his title, but I did, as a child, read *The Houseboat on the Styx*—a *jeu d'esprit* (author unknown) in which dead people sit around talking across the centuries. I loved that book and it was probably from it that I got the idea for a game I used to play, a habit I developed of talking to Charlotte Brontë. After a year spent in Wales with my mother's cousins, I returned to Alabama, made sick at heart by suburban dullness. I tried to recapture the magic of the Welsh countryside, exploring until I'd found a creek with willows—an Ophelia creek—skirting the fields where the Alabama State Cavalry pastured its horses. Charlotte Brontë and I used to take walks there and my game was to figure out what I would have to explain to her, what was different in my time and place. And the answer was, of

Read at the Spring, 1988, meeting of the New Society for Language and Rhetoric, University of Illinois, Chicago. First published In *Discurrendo*, the newsletter of the Society.

course, almost everything . . . except one evening, suddenly the
sky glowed red—the open hearth furnaces out in Bessemer were
being cooled down over the weekend—and I remarked, "Well,
Charlotte, THAT will be familiar!" Later—much later—it occurred to me that the mills familiar to Charlotte Brontë were
not steel mills!

Those imaginary conversations were good practice in developing what Kenneth Burke calls "perspective by incongru-
ity." Fifty years later, on the occasion of my retirement, I played
a version of the old game. I preached a sermon: text—several
of them—explications, exemplifications, and exhortation. We
concluded with a Hymn to Rhetoric. My sermon was organized
as an extended metaphor of battle, a topography in which conventional rhetorical forces were set upon by Freire's guerrillas,
and Richards' reinforcements, with Schleiermacher surveying
the field, looking across to Mt. Peirce. I believe in Kenneth
Burke's motto, *Ad bellum purificandum*, which does not mean,
as Professor Kinneavy apparently thinks, "Let's have a good
fight which will clear the air," but rather "Advance toward the
purification of the war." The war is the human condition; it
is the consequence of the Fall, but we can purify conflict, work
so that it is not murderous. What I'm reading today is a further
effort at purification by talk.

And finally, in this list of origins, let me note that I have
always loved allegory as a mode of discourse since it allows
the dialectic of emblem and narrative to shape ideas. I can't
claim that that actually happens in what I've written—the
shaping, I mean—but perhaps the ideas will peek through.

My plan is to decode the title and to introduce the speak-
ers before we listen in on what they are saying. First the decoding, in the form of an interpretive paraphrase: *Ramus meets
Schleiermacher and they go off for a triadic lunch with Peirce;
Vico drops by.*

Rhetoric—insofar as it has anything to do with teaching
—must engage hermeneutics in order to find a place for interpretation. That will require a semiotic underpinning, but the
theory of signs must be of a certain sort. It must be a triadic
semiotics—a theory of signification in which interpretation is
constitutive, not additive; interpretation must be seen as the
*logical condition for the making of meaning, not a psycholog-
ical accident.*

In Peirce's philosophy of representation, meaning is a three-valued, not a two-valued relationship. In my opinion, what we have in postmodern, deconstructionist, poststructuralist thought is a criticism shot through with dyadic conceptions, a criticism which is trying to come to grips with triadic formulations— and NOT succeeding. A triadic semiotics will allow us to develop, at last, a logic of the humanities, free of that pseudo-science which worships the Idols of the Laboratory.

My interpretive paraphrase is beginning to need interpretation, so let me turn to the gazetteer which will identify my protagonists.

Petrus Ramus (Pierre de la Ramée), 1515–1572. Killed on St. Bartholomew's Day—the Massacre of Huguenots; led to his being called a martyr, by Christopher Marlowe and Increase Mather, among others. But he may have been murdered by assassins hired by his chief academic rival, Jacques Charpentier (Charpentrius). Ramist dialectic swept Europe, especially important in England and with the American Puritans.

The chief source of information for modern rhetoricians seems to be Walter J. Ong, S. J. Ramist dialectic was centrally important for the New England Mind, which Father Ong studied in Perry Miller's seminar at Harvard, just after the war. A decade later he published *Ramus, Method, and the Decay of Dialogue.* Most rhetoricians parrot what they find in this book, which bears on its title page an epigram from Justus Lipsius:

> Young man, listen to me: you will never be a great man
> if you think that Ramus was a great man.

For Father Ong, the Reformation was an aberration and Ramus's attempts to make method accessible, an affront to the privileged clergy. For another perspective, I've turned to Miller and to Rosemond Tuve, whose *Elizabethan and Metaphysical Imagery* remains the best study of Renaissance poetics. (It was admiringly reviewed by Kenneth Burke in 1948; I've never seen it mentioned by any rhetorician in the past forty years.)

Friedrich Daniel Ernst Schleiermacher, 1768–1834. Born a Moravian and remained close to those Pietist roots all his life. Trained as a philologist. Came to Biblical texts with a well-developed method which was linguistically sophisticated and historically sound. Developed a method of exegesis which he set forth as a model for a general theory of hermeneutics. He's best known for *empathy (Einfühlung)* and the hermeneutic circle because both were stressed by his champion, Wilhelm Dilthey. I have depended on essays by Richard Niebuhr and Karl Barth and on my reading of Schleiermacher's *Monologen*.

Charles Sanders Peirce, 1839–1914. Enjoyed a long life— though "enjoyed" is not quite the word since he lived in terrible, not even genteel, poverty for decades. A friend of mine used to say that there was a grim significance in the fact that America allowed her greatest philosopher to starve to death. Not too far from the truth. Richard Martin, a founder of the Peirce Society, used to say that "Charlie Peirce" was right up there with Plato and Leibnitz as one of the greatest philosophers of all time . . . this, on the basis of his logic. Richard Rorty, on the other hand, has stated that the *only* importance of Peirce is that he influenced William James: that tells us quite a bit about Richard Rorty.

Let me note that what you need to know here about Peirce is that his semiotic is based on a triadic conception of the sign. Saussure, you know, developed his semiology in *dyadic* terms: a signifier and a signified. For Peirce, the meaning relationship is necessarily *triadic* because interpretation is the logical condition for signification. If you can visualize—or *draw*—a triangle with a dotted line as the base, you will have an emblem of triadic semiotics. (This triangle appears in Ogden and Richards' *The Meaning of Meaning*, 1923.) A symbol—or *representamen*—stands for its *object*, its *referent*, only by means of a meaning, an idea which we hold in mind, a reference, an *interpretant*—not an interpreter: Peirce's semiotics makes interpretation a logical, not a psychological element of the sign. (I tell *you* this now so that *Peirce* doesn't have to explain to his visitors.)

Giambattista Vico, 1668–1744. Vico was 32 before the eighteenth century opened: It is not the age of reason which should claim him so much as the age of *duplex veritas*: "double truth" came in with science. He was a rhetorician, but *I* would prefer to call him the first philosophical anthropologist. He sought to make the study of language the model for the history of institutions and in that sense he was the intellectual forebear of Edward Sapir. Michelet and Croce introduced Vico to historians. Bill Covino has done an excellent job of reminding modern rhetoricians of his great richness. People of my generation were often introduced to Vico via James Joyce! *Finnegans Wake* begins in the middle of a sentence, the first part of which constitutes the conclusion of the book, an emblem of

Vico's concept of *ricorso* and punning on this term: ". . . by a commodious vicus of recirculation . . ." Ernst Cassirer remains the most interesting guide to Vico. In his *Logic of the Humanities*, he sees Vico as the philosopher who understood what the study of man entails—a study of his works, his institutions, his language: Vico's new science concerns not God's creation but man's. I have also turned to Max Fisch, a philosopher who is as well acquainted with Vico as he is with Peirce. He hears the eternal concords.

In the process of composing this imaginary conversation, I discovered many untoward parallels and many surprising dissimilarities. The composing process was so intensely heuristic that it just about wrecked my enterprise and it certainly slowed it down. Here are two examples of how finding out more changed the drift and the configurations.

Originally I had Ramus say, "The waters of the Seine were very cold on St. Bartholomew's Day when they closed over my head." And Schleiermacher says: "I *feel* for you." I soon discovered that Ramus was killed by defenestration; his broken body was seized down below and decapitated, hacked up, and thrown into the Seine in pieces. My original image was downright sentimental, in view of what actually happened. Furthermore, I had thought that the only real point about the confrontation of Schleiermacher and Ramus would be that one was a taxonomist and the other a Romantic for whom feeling was crucial. But I discovered, of course, that *method* is the point at which their differences can be most clearly illuminated.

Perry Miller and Rosemond Tuve both stress that Ramist method makes axiom more important than syllogism, that axiom was seen to be consonant with Adam's unfallen, single vision—"single" there in the good sense of directly coming from God and having no need for dialectic. Looking again at *The Gutenberg Galaxy*, for the first time in twenty years, I find that McLuhan claims that adage, proverb, aphorism, "sentence," exemplum, etc., are all essential to an oral culture—which is then allied with *wisdom*, in contradistinction to *commerce*! McLuhan does not call the oral culture an *illiterate* one, nor does he recognize the role of axiom (which can be just as nonlinear as adage) in Ramist thought.

There are startling parallels and divergences in the lives and ideas of these four figures. As you juxtapose them in different ways, new alliances form, new ruptures appear. Ramus and Vico frame the Renaissance; Schleiermacher and Peirce frame the modern era—and yet Vico and Peirce would have more to say to one another, perhaps, than either would to his near contemporary. There is a big gap—the seventeenth century—which obviously should have been represented by Francis Bacon. And I found myself planning other encounters, all along the way: Coleridge and Cusanus take a midnight canoe ride; Rosemond Tuve and Susanne Langer have Sunday brunch; Owen Barfield drops by. Ross Winterowd and Vince Ruggiero go on a camping trip; Walker Percy, disguised as a grizzly bear, chases them over a cliff. (Professor John Edward Hardy suggested to me that this should have been a fishing trip, with Walker Percy in an alligator suit.)

Among the four we will hear from on this occasion, we may note the following commonalities:

1. They are *all* fundamentally and passionately concerned with method.
2. *All* acknowledge the centrality of learning—all were teachers at one time or another, though Peirce only briefly, but pedagogy was for them *all* a matter of philosophical and political importance.
3. *All* recognize the role of spirit in human affairs and are intensely concerned with the definition of man—of human life.
4. *All* display—though I'm uncertain about Ramus—what I call a typological imagination: they search for representations of general truths; such representation is the principal aim of their rhetoric, hermeneutics, semiotics, and logic.
5. And, finally, none of the four is read, actually read: Ramus wrote in Latin and French; Schleiermacher in German, of course; Peirce wrote in Peirce-ese, and Vico in Italian. But it isn't just the barrier of foreign languages which makes access difficult; they aren't read in translation either! The reason is, I think, a habit which has developed of academicizing everything so that we are content to have "messages" at second-hand—third- and fourth-hand. Academics are less likely to read Peirce than they are to read Terence Hawkes—or Robert Scholes redacting what Hawkes reports on the basis of his reading of Derrida attempting to understand Peirce. A good bit of what you will be overhearing in *these* exchanges was actually said in *some* language on *some* occasion by the speaker.

We come upon Ramus and Schleiermacher walking along the river in the city of Jena.

s: Ramus, I must admit to a certain jealousy about the times you lived in, how they worked to your advantage. Your rhetoric or dialectic—and I must admit I do not always understand those terms as you and your followers used them—your *Institutes* were received as an important adjunct to the new science and the new religion, but by my time, science needed no help from rhetoric and it did not know that it needed a hermeneutic! Religion was certainly in decline; indeed, I felt compelled to compose a defense of religion against the attacks of its cultured despisers.

r: It was not religion which interested me, really. In any case, Protestantism is more than a religion. My dialectic was intended to clear out the medieval undergrowth or, rather, the thickets which had been deliberately cultivated by those who meant some people to be kept out. All the intricate taxonomies and procedural guides which served as instruments of the Church's tyranny. Those redactions produced my single method and that is what caught on. My concern was not religion per se but education.

s: I never saw them as a dichotomy. But pardon me: I realize how important dichotomy is to your way of thinking. For me, homiletics and pedagogy are on a continuum, and method and purpose are dialectical, and the individual and his society are in dialogue and . . .

r: My principle of *use* takes care of all that. But it is method which is crucial, not continua or what you strangely call "hermeneutic."

s: Isn't it true, Ramus, that method is what people don't understand?

r: My method was very well understood and that was because it was founded on the natural light of reason. Any man can find his own way by using my method. I made it possible for every man to think methodically. One fiery-faced Aristotelian expressed the dismay this caused: "Every cobbler can cob a syllogism."

S: Aristotelians have never understood that syllogisms are devices for getting from one intuition to another. Intuition is an act of mind.

R: It is the natural light of reason which makes this possible and my single method which *realizes* it, in our French sense of bringing to pass, of making manifest. The new rhetoric is not guileful persuasion but the logic of tropes and schemes. Poets who read my *Institutes* thus learned to argue in their verses and that tough reasonableness created a new poetry and a new "grace." I illustrated my principles—my institutes—with poetry and the poets rediscovered their art. Later priests have complained that I killed rhetoric by removing invention from its purview, but that is a Jesuitical argument. What I did was, in effect, to *enlarge* the domain of rhetoric: what I claimed was that insofar as rhetoric concerns invention, it is a matter of logic. And when I left *style* to rhetoric, I didn't mean mere window dressing.

S: Was your method not concerned with interpretation?

R: Interpretation? That was not a speculative instrument in my day. My concern was pedagogical, not philosophical. I wanted to regularize method and of course the privileged clerics who knew how to work their way through the undergrowth, those Aristotelian tangles—*they* were on the defensive.

S: I too had a method and a pedagogy: I think this always is true of Protestants: it's the good side of the self-righteousness which we always risk.

R: Even self-righteousness—and I know nothing of that—is not as bad as laziness. Pedagogues in my time wanted to be able to teach automatically and they used the syllogism to let them do that.

S: How familiar that is! Even our Luther yielded to that attitude when he declared that catechisms were necessary because of ill-educated ministers, but I saw no excuse for ill-educated ministers! And from what you say, Ramus, you wanted to address that problem of illiteracy more directly.

R: Priests fear literacy of all degrees; orality allows them to remain in control, to exercise the sacraments as their means of enslavement. The sacrament of Confession is an institution which glorifies orality. I wanted to free man by having him use his eyes.

S: A reading congregation will have no need of catechisms. I argued that if we *had* to have them—and you know the strength of habit—each minister should compose his own, and should do so each day!

R: Ha! That is the kind of subversion which would have had you massacred in Paris in 1572! But it is method, precisely, which recreates the clergy and the congregation, as well as the teacher and his pupils. But what was your method? How did you go about supplanting catechism?

S: Hymnody! Singing together I considered the best emblem of community, a certain strengthener of Faith, a way to enact and express feeling. (Schleiermacher, seeing that Ramus is dumbfounded, quickly adds) But I also developed a method of reading that is my hermeneutics, which I also developed as a general theory of critical inquiry.

My method—my hermeneutics—was twofold but not sequential. I held that grammatical construction was in a dialectical relationship with a psychological understanding. We begin with misunderstandings and proceed by building historical and stylistic contexts. This comparative method I had learned in my study of the Platonic dialogues and developed it in my theories of exegesis. But, just as the grammatical and the psychological work together, so the comparative approach is inescapably related to what I called the *divinatory* mode. My champion was Dilthey—I have not had legions of champions, as you have had, Ramus—but he meant something by science which I did not really mean by my method. He forgot the emphasis I put on the interdependence, the *ineinander* of the modes of interpretation.

R: I recognize that problem, for when I differentiated analysis and genesis, I did not mean that as a difference in essence but only as a pedagogical sequence. We have to begin somewhere and I held that we should begin with reading, not writing, with analysis of propositions as they have been constructed, and then turn to genesis, the construction of propositions.

s: I agree about the pedagogical imperative, but I think it should be an unquestioned premise that we begin with our students where they are and that is as historical creatures and as children of the Lord. The universal and essential point of departure is *feeling* because the feeling of dependence on the Lord is a universal experience.

r: I do not follow that particular line, but I certainly hold that the natural light of reason will lead us to God and *that* is what logic is *for*: true logic is in correspondence with the laws of nature. The mind and nature are in correspondence, and that is why we can be logical and that is why there can be a *single* method.

s: I am somewhat more interested in *human* nature. Every creation of the human mind can be examined and comprehended from two points of view. You can look at it from its inner essence, and then see it as a product of human nature, grounded in one of man's necessary ways of behavior, or instincts. Or you can look at it from its circumference with reference to the determinate form it has assumed in various times and places; then you see it as a product of time and history.

r: Your dichotomy is not mine, but at least we agree that the student must proceed methodically and that that method will succeed because of reason and its instrument which is logic.

s: Well, no I can't agree that logic is the primary instrument. Feeling, the divinatory mode, the intuition of inner form—all that is what I would claim is essential, but then I have the benefit of another age. My friend Herder's concept of inner form was simply not available to you. And the doctrine of inner form is profoundly related to the centrality of the study of language, which emerged more than a hundred years after your time. What we need, I think, if we are to explore the relationship of form and method, is a talk with a philosopher in America.

r: Certainly the Americans were friendly to *my* method. Will we be going to Harvard? The seal of that great in-

stitution is, you know, VERITAS, the slogan of the Ra-
mists.

S: Our philosopher was born in Cambridge and was educated
at Harvard, but we will find him now in Pennyslvania.
He's agreed to receive us and in fact has invited us to
lunch, so we should hurry.

When Schleiermacher and Ramus arrive in Milford,
Pennsylvania, they have no trouble finding Peirce's house,
which is a rather decayed mansion on top of a hill over-
looking the countryside. But finding Peirce is another
matter. When there's no answer at the front door, they go
around to the back of the house, where they find Mrs.
Peirce in the vegetable garden. She explains that Peirce is
in the attic and that they should go there to meet him.
And she pushes a button and a rope ladder slowly descends. The Europeans are surprised, but they think, these
Americans have odd ways.

Peirce calls from the top of the ladder encouragingly
and helps first Ramus and then Schleiermacher to the
landing.

P: I regret that I must ask you to rely on this mode of ascent.
It is here that I hide from my creditors and since nobody
else ever visits me, it hadn't occurred to me that this could
be difficult. However, you are here. I must say that I have
been hesitant about meeting philosophers who are theo-
logians: indeed, I have claimed that the reason that philosophy has for so long been without an adequate method
is that philosophers have come more generally from the
seminary than from the laboratory.

R: Monsieur, I am not a theologian. I am a rhetorician.

P: That's no better—unless of course you mean by rhetoric
something other than the study of moldy ornament. Or
shiny ornament. There are many senses of "rhetoric" and
I have spent much of my time in distinguishing speculative rhetoric from other kinds ... of defining the relationship of rhetoric to method, of method to the method
we might devise for developing methods, of exploring the
relationship of method to the ongoing process of inter-

pretation which I call *semiosis*, in contradistinction, of course, to my semiotics. On the other hand . . . (Ramus looks back over his shoulder to see if the ladder is still in place, but it has been swallowed up by some mechanism. There is to be no easy escape. He decides to put as good a face on things as he can.)

R: Is this your ivory tower? I had thought you were a man of the world.

P: I have in my time been a man of the world. I worked with the geodetic survey; I traveled with my father, the mathematician Benjamin Peirce, to Sicily to witness and measure certain effects of a solar eclipse from atop Mt. Etna and also to test certain calculations I had made about the pendulum. I am a scientist and a logician and that is tantamount to being of this world, but the academy had no room for me. I lost my position because disgruntled colleagues reported my unconventional living arrangements to the authorities.

R: My fate was somewhat more dramatic: academic malice cost me not a position but my life.

S: I was more fortunate, having a generous disposition, and I never enjoyed disputatiousness. One of my most startling essays was set forth as a genial Dialogue on Christmas Eve. And I preached each Sunday and managed to reach my congregation. . . .

R: Yes, yes, we know: through hymn singing!

S: Ah, my dear Ramus, you have forgotten the rationale, which is that singing brings people together and that community is essential for the apprehension of one's historical being.

P: Well, that is a very interesting argument. I have always claimed that the process of signification goes on in a community constituted by those for whom it makes a difference that it should go on.

R: I see no need for such a vague idea as "community": my method was useful because any one person could use it. Indeed, one of the Puritan divines here in America translated the basic principles of my dialectic into Algonquin.

Dividing, sowing asunder: that is a power of reason which all men share.

P: Yes, I know you were a great man for dichotomy. Different numbers have found their champions. *Five* was extolled by Sir Thomas Browne and as all the world knows you extolled *Two*, Ramus. I am forced to confess to a leaning to the number *Three* in philosophy. As for dividing, I rather like the psychological definition of Cicero which you adopted, Ramus: *Dialecta est ars se tradere bene disserendi*. The pun is useful: disputing and sowing, dispersion. Gerundives suggest process, but they only suggest, they do not represent: it is logic, not rhetoric, which is the philosophy of representation.

R: But you forget that my method did just that. By simply looking at the schemata in my manuals, the student could *see* how propositions should be related, or, rather, how sentences are related. My followers were not interested in deductions; they wanted to preach in sentences. They learned to depend not on syllogisms but on axioms. Since the laws of the mind are absolutely the same as the laws of nature, if the laws are laid out in axiomatic fashion, then the method will be there on the page. My genius was that I simplified a procedure which could be visually represented; my method would have been impossible without Gutenberg! My distributions could be represented typographically, thus freeing men from the tyranny of orality, of illiteracy which in a sense was rife in the universities of my time.

S: I can't believe that Jesus Christ Our Lord would have been content with publishing tracts!

P: That is a point which we need to clarify. The dichotomy which Ramus is making between the oral and the graphic representation of the oral is crucial. The point of representation is a much more complex matter, for we are capable of understanding representations only by having conceptions or mental representations which represent the given representation as a representation.

S: *Peirce*! that is unintelligible, I must say!

P: I fear you are right. I am so unused to thinking in words that I sometimes land in swamps of unintelligibility. What

I mean is that we are capable of recognizing signs only by having conceptions or mental forms—schema, images, diagrams—which make possible that recognition by offering the grounds of analogy between a situation, or an image or idea, and our remembrance of it. In short—but I do not know how to be short—our method must include a method of method, just as our representations are always *of* representations. My existential graphs were an attempt to make spatial form carry logical relationships, much as a *metaphora* carries meaning, but in any case, tables are not method: there is no room for returning to premises by abduction; there is no role for the critic in mere taxonomic tables.

R: A method should preclude the necessity of interpretation. God's law is represented in the natural reason of man: if we depend on axioms regarding the self-evident, we will be able, by carefully ordering them, to return to Adamic right reason, a prelapsarian ability to think immediately without the help of syllogisms. My logic holds that the primary function of thinking is not investigation and deduction but discerning and disposing.

P: No taxonomy can do the work of semiosis. Science is not taxonomy, though of course that discovery was not part of your time. Philosophers persist in building theories in which they leave out thirdness.

R: Thirdness? That sounds Aristotelian to me.

P: I don't believe I can explain my categories before lunch, but let me say that Thirdness is what drives all reasoning, all inference. My method, which I called abduction, has proved essential to science, especially when what the scientist is investigating cannot be seen. I instituted hypotheticals in order to keep all suppositions tentative and clearly subject to interpretation.

S: I feel that we should continue after lunch, but I don't mean to be hasty. (Peirce seems embarrassed and he mumbles a bit, but pretty soon they are seated at the table, each with a plate of dandelion greens. But just as they start to eat, they hear a strain of Vivaldi whistled from below the open windows. Peirce jumps up and runs to see.)

P: VICO! You've *returned!*

V: (from below) As is my wont. But you will need to help me with the ladder. (Peirce lets down the ladder, descends, and returns bearing a couple of large flat cartons; Vico follows with several more. Peirce introduces Vico to Ramus and Schleiermacher and then Vico speaks.)

V: I have brought some Neapolitan pizza; it is the best in the world, you know.

And while Peirce is getting the wine, he whispers to Ramus and Schleiermacher, "I know that otherwise one might not find one's hunger satisfied." Schleiermacher offers to summarize the discussion so far and does so. Vico then responds:

V: I had hoped to find that Peirce had invited Bacon, if not Plato, Tacitus, or Grotius, but I am delighted to meet a fellow rhetorician and a fellow student of language. Let me say that the notion of teaching by means of axiom is part of my scheme: we can reclaim mankind's earliest forms of reasoning, making them our own again. What I call the poetic wisdom of early man, man in the early ages, allows us access to some truths otherwise hidden from us. And your hermeneutics, Schleiermacher, seems consonant with my search for the providential history of man and as you have probably discovered, it certainly is with *il professore's* doctrine of the interpretant.

S: Vico, you were a man before your time.

V: That's what they always say. I've been called Europe's somnambulist, dreaming my method, my philosophy of society, in advance of my time. You and Ramus appeared when the time was propitious; Peirce and I have had to wait for a new day.

S: Well, the new day came very quickly and prepared for your rediscovery: The *ricorso di Vico* should gratify Vico! What I mean is that it was less than a hundred years after your time when Jakob Grimm and his brother undertook their study of the German language, an enterprise which like yours was motivated by an interest in the concept of nationhood. Grimm invented a Northern version of your *poetic imagination*; or, put it this way: he realized that the tales he heard and recorded represented the history of the language and he thought that that history would reveal the secret of the German Volk.

R: (coming to life) The art of finding secrets is the secret art of Renaissance rhetoric. We look for what is hidden; that's why rhetoric was a secret art and an art of secrets. One of my English followers called arguments *foxes* and places, their *burrows*: the rhetor is a *hunter* who locates arguments, who runs them to earth, who ferrets or hounds those foxes out of their burrows.

P: (coolly) That conception is entirely inadequate for any scientific enterprise.

V: OR historical enterprise: a method must account for process, for growth, for history.

S: Surely we all agree that whatever the enterprise, it is hermeneutic. We all must diagnose, and when the hunter unleashes his hounds, is that not a kind of diagnosis? We are all hermeneuts; we all find, though our findings may have different origins.

R: My single method provides the procedures.

P: *But it cannot provide for its own critique!* And you do not acknowledge chance in the universe. If everything ran according to schedule, as you have it, there would be no chance of novelty, nor yet of growth.

S: We understand one another best when that fundamental metaphor of growth and development is apprehended; Vico, you are an honorary Protestant, but we will need to find other ground on which we can meet Ramus. (But Ramus has retired to the far end of the attic and is sound asleep.)

V: I do not mind being called an honorary Romantic, but I don't wish to be an honorary Protestant, despite the fact that I and my friends occasionally suffered at the hands of The Inquisition. Protestantism forgets community, forgets the *gentes*, ignores the nations.

S: Ah, my friend, that is not so! I was a Prussian and my constant aim was to enliven the imagination of my congregations to what it meant to be a Prussian. Your work recognizes the dialectic of freedom and fate, I believe. And it should do the same for individual and nation. It is our

aim to make Destiny our choice; *Virtù* is precisely that
which makes possible the workings of Providence, makes
it manifest in human history . . . and history is the activity
of the human spirit.

v: Precisely so! That is why I have insisted that it is man's
work, his life in history, which should be the subject of
the new science. God's creation can only truly be known
by God; what man can know is his history, his institutions, the means by which he has constituted himself a
social being. My principle of *verum factum* enunciates
this claim. I was concerned not with *the truth* but with
the true: specificity is the essential focus of rhetoric, in
contradistinction to metaphysics. I spoke of *vera*—the
trues—and claimed that we must seek these trues among
what we have made—our human inventions and institutions.

p: As I have often observed, Vico, if you had relied on the
Greek term rather than the Latin, you'd have more easily
stressed the prospective, the social, the transcendental
sense of the true. Futurity, man! If you had taken one
more step, you'd have come to the concept of probability
and that consequent ability to ask "What would be the
effect or the operation of such and such?" In short, you'd
have reached my pragmaticism. In any case, all who seek
to answer the riddle of the Sphinx will need the guidance
of a science of signs. And of course we must always acknowledge that Man is himself a Sign. Each sign requires
another for its interpretation; therefore each man requires
the presence and the activity of other men, other signs.

s: That dialectic of interpretation and representation is precisely what I intended my hermeneutics to enlighten.

v: And it is that articulation which makes us fully human:
our laws are but our habits institutionalized and our habits are determined by our history. (Peirce is clearly ready
to begin a disquisition on habit, but Schleiermacher heads
him off.)

s: Here is the ground of our meeting: we all see the human
creature as divine, whether we mean "created by the Lord"
or a diviner, a seeker after Truth—or the trues. And we
see each human being as a person, an individual, *and* as

a member of a community, whether we call it a *gens*, a nation, a congregation, or a class.

V: Whatever it is, the larger unit is given shape and is defined by its institutions, not only by its jurisprudence but by literature: the tales we tell, the kinds of poems we write, the songs we sing, the dreams we attend to—they are all *signs*. Is that a proper use of the term, Peirce? And we never lose that capacity for metaphor.

P: It is indeed rare to hear someone who recognizes metaphor as a mode of thought, not as a rhetorical ornament. Metaphor is analogy and analogy is the chief form abduction takes.

V: We could quibble over "ornament"—and I'm sure Ramus would do so—but I take your meaning because, of course, it is mine: my theory of the descent of man features the idea that poetry is a form of knowledge, that myths are our first philosophy.

P: And mathematics our last, though I consider algebra a kind of vision, not unlike perception itself. But all our representations, all man's works are our proper concern.

S: They have a form *divine*.

V: We all agree, noting your ambiguity carefully.

P: Our representations are made by persons, but *they* are never merely individual: we know that man is not whole as long as he is single, that he is essentially a possible member of society. Especially, one man's experience is nothing if it stands alone. If he sees what others cannot, we call it hallucination. But then society I consider in the figure of a *loosely compacted person*! Schleiermacher, will you please compose our manifesto?

S: I will gladly do so. It seems to me . . . or shall I speak for us all? We hold that each man is meant to represent humanity in his own way, combining its elements uniquely, so that it may reveal itself in every mode, and all that can issue from its womb be made actual in the fullness of unending space and time.

V: Go and wake up Ramus! He must sign this as well. And I am sure he *will*, if we can make some divisions and sow a bit asunder!

Works Cited

(Note: Essays which have been reprinted in *Reclaiming the Imagination* are cited parenthetically in the text. Original sources are given in *Reclaiming*.)

Arnheim, Rudolf, *Art and Visual Perception* (Berkeley: University of California, 1954).
_____*Visual Thinking* (Berkeley: University of California, 1969).
Ashton-Warner, Sylvia, *Teacher* (London: Secker & Warburg, 1963).
_____*Spearpoint* (New York: Knopf, 1972).
Bamberger, Jeanne, "The Art of Cognitive Risk Taking," *Papers from Invitational Conference on Innovation and Productivity in Higher Education* (San Francisco: San Francisco Press, 1977).
Berthoff, Ann E., *Forming/Thinking/Writing* (Second Edition with James Stephens), (Portsmouth, NH: Boynton/Cook, 1988).
_____*The Making of Meaning: Metaphors, Models, and Maxims for Writing Teachers* (Portsmouth, NH: Boynton/Cook, 1981).
_____*Reclaiming the Imagination: Philosophical Perspectives for Writers and Teachers of Writing*) (Portsmouth, NH: Boynton/Cook, 1984).
_____"I. A. Richards and the Audit of Meaning," *New Literary History*, 13 (Fall, 1982), 63–79.
_____"I. A. Richards," in *Traditions of Inquiry*, ed. John C. Brereton (New York: Oxford University Press, 1985).
_____"Sapir and the Two Tasks of Language," *Semiotica*, 71-1/2 (1988), 1–47.
Borroff, Marie, "Computer as Poet," *Yale Alumni Magazine*, January 1971.
_____"Creativity, Poetic Language, and the Computer," *The Yale Review*, LX (1971), 481–513.

169

170   *Works Cited*

Brooks, Phyllis, "Mimesis: Grammar and the Echoing Voice," *College English* 35 (November. 1973), 161–68.

Burke, Kenneth, *Permanence and Change* (1934; Indianapolis: Bobbs-Merrill, 1965).

Cassirer, Ernst, *Essay on Man* (New Haven: Yale University Press, 1944).

Cole, Michael and Scribner, Sylvia, "Literacy Without Schooling: Testing for Intellectual Effects," *Harvard Educational Review*, 48 (1978), 448–61.

Donaldson, Margaret, *Children's Minds* (New York: Norton, 1979).

Freedman, Aviva and Pringle, Ian, "Writing in the College Years," *CCC*, 31 (October 1980), 311–24.

Freire, Paulo, *The Politics of Education* (South Hadley, MA: Bergin & Garvey, 1985).

———*The Pedagogy of the Oppressed* (New York: Herder & Herder, 1970).

Freisinger, Randall, "Cross-Disciplinary Writing Workshops: Theory and Practice," *College English*, 42 (1980), 154–66.

Geertz, Clifford, *The Interpretation of Cultures* (New York: Basic Books, 1973).

Langer, Susanne K., *Problems of Art* (New York: Scribner's, 1957).

———*Philosophical Sketches* (Baltimore, MD: Johns Hopkins, 1962).

Lewis, C. S., *An Experiment in Criticism* (Cambridge: Cambridge Univ Press, 1963).

Miles, Josephine, *Working Out Ideas: Predication and Other Uses of Language* (Berkeley: Bay Area Writing Project, Curriculum Publication No. 5, 1979).

Miller, Susan, "Rhetorical Maturity: Definition and Development," in *Reinventing the Rhetorical Tradition*, ed. Aviva Freedman and Ian Pringle (Conway, Ark: L & S Books, 1980).

Oppenheimer, J. Robert, *The Open Mind* (New York: Simon & Schuster, 1949).

Percy, Walker, *Lost in the Cosmos: The Last Self-Help Book* (New York: Farrar, Straus & Giroux, 1983).

Richards, I. A., *Practical Criticism* (1929; New York: Harcourt, 1965).

———*The Philosophy of Rhetoric* (1936; New York: Oxford University Press, 1965).

———*Speculative Instruments* (New York: Harcourt, 1955).

———*So Much Nearer* (New York: Harcourt, 1960).

———*Design for Escape* (New York: Harcourt, 1968).

———*The Written Word* (with Sheridan Baker and Jacques Barzun) (Rowley, MA: Newbury House, 1971).

Rosenblatt, Louise R., *Literature as Exploration* (New York: Appleton-Century-Croft, 1938).

———*The Reader, The Text and The Poem* (Carbondale: Southern Illinois University Press, 1978).

———"Whitman's Democratic Vistas and the New 'Ethnicity,' " *The Yale Review*, 67 (1978).

Salvatori, Mariolina, "The Pedagogical Implications of Reader-Response Theory," *Reader*, 16 (1986), 1–19.

Vygotsky, L. S., *Thought and Language* (Cambridge, MA: MIT Press, 1962).

_____*Mind in Society* (Cambridge, MA: Harvard Univ. Press, 1978).

Wall, Susan V. and Petrosky, Anthony R., "Freshman Writers and Revision: Results from a Survey," *Journal of Basic Writing*, 3 (Fall/Winter, 1981).

Wilson, John, *Thinking with Concepts* (Cambridge: Cambridge University Press, 1963).